BITING BITING

KITCHEN
PRESS

For my Tone, Amber Priya and Amy Sienna
#famgether

BITING BITING

BITING

Snacking Gujarati-style

Urvashi Roe

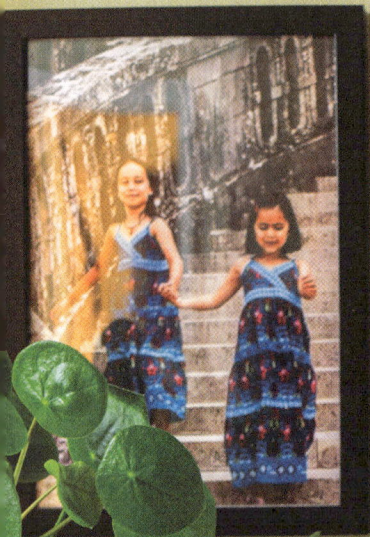

CONTENTS

I am a firm believer in understanding where you've come from to move forwards into the future. I believe that, like a classic recipe which has core ingredients, there are core 'ingredients' to our personalities which are embedded. Sometimes it's really clear where they come from. Other times they don't make any sense because nobody in your immediate family does things that way – or at least as far as you know, but when you dig deeper back into the past you unravel stories from the older generations that link it all together and suddenly it all adds up.

My story starts in Dodoma, Tanzania in 1970. That's where I was born. It was a small village back then, not the industrial town it has now become. I don't remember much. Through photos I can recall never being without my Mr India toy; playing in the garden with my first cousin Dina; eating mangoes; the boat made of seashells on a shelf in our living room. Small glimpses of what seemed a happy life. I also remember lots of guns and soldiers. Military cars zooming past our house. More on that later.

I always wondered how I came to be born in Tanzania. I get asked this question a lot but our elders have passed and we rely on the fading memories of our parents, uncles and aunties to help piece it all together. Photos trigger smiles of days gone by.

In the 1930s and 40s, the last-but-one generation of my family made their way from India to what was then known by the British as Tanganyika Territory. My maternal grandfather was the first, travelling on a dhow from Gujarat and landing on the shores of Zanzibar. He had itchy feet, was adventurous and enterprising and, reading between the lines of the stories I've heard, it seems

like he ran away from home to make a new life for himself. After some time in Zanzibar he travelled all over Africa doing different jobs before settling in Tanzania and establishing himself as a mechanic with garages first in Lindi and then Dar es Salaam, Tanga and Arusha. He got married to my maternal grandmother – my Baa – and raised a family of eight. Three sons and five daughters. I don't remember him much at all. I know he was besotted with me because I was a good girl. Obedient, quiet and quick to learn rather than noisy, mischievous or a cry baby like some of my cousins.

On the other side of my family, my paternal grandfather uprooted his whole family to Tanzania in 1947 when my father was just five years old. The family all had British citizenship so he got a permit visa to work, seeing better opportunities there than in India where there was growing unrest after Independence. Settling

Facing page: Mota Bapa and Mota Baa circa 1940

Left: Mum and Dad circa 1965

in Dodoma was not planned. On their way from Dar es Salaam to Tabora on the train, the family met an old friend from Gujarat who encouraged them to stay in Dodoma and set up a garage there. It seems they took his advice and stayed, setting up Remtulla Garage and a couple of others before returning to India to retire in the early 1960s.

Dad remained in Tanzania and lived with his elder brother, my Govind Bapa. After finishing school he found a career in banking and the pressure was on to find a good wife. His marriage was arranged in 1967, when Mum was only twenty and Dad twenty-five. She'd barely left school and thought Dad looked like Cliff Richard. He wanted a family-minded life partner who would be happy to send money back home to his parents. So that was that. A perfect match. I was born in 1970 and I don't think I was put down until my sisters came along. Growing up in an extended family meant that there was always someone to hold me and look after me whether I was sleeping or needed to play. This was seen as the norm and indeed when my eldest daughter was born my mum was aghast when I put her down once in the laundry basket while I did the washing up. It took a while to explain that I didn't have the luxury of aunts, sisters-in-law and cousins on hand to look after the baby's every whim.

Life for my parents seemed to be good. There are many photos of us travelling in Lake Manyara, in N'gorongoro Crater and to the seaside in Dar es Salaam. Their siblings were marrying and having

their own children. Lots of family gatherings, temple visits and community functions. But African nationalisation was starting to take hold. Idi Amin had overthrown the government in Uganda just north of Tanzania, and family there were becoming unsettled and leaving to go back to India or elsewhere. The same political unrest was starting to take hold in Kenya and quickly spreading southwards to Tanzania and Zambia.

Govind Bapa was the first to return to India with his family. It must have been around 1972 as I was about 18 months old. Mum and I travelled with them and all their luggage on the boat into Bombay. It didn't hit me that I would have arrived into the Gateway of India back then until I did a walking tour of the area in 2019. The guide was talking about the boat loads of returnees and I stopped dead in my tracks, thinking about my toddler self on this huge cargo boat. I don't remember that visit at all but there are many photos of me hoisted up on my paternal grandfather's shoulder and sitting on his lap playing with my toys. My dad was due to travel with us too but there was a last-minute issue with his paperwork and so he ended up flying over. Reading between the lines I think this trip was to seek my grandfather's blessing to travel to England.

In April 1976 my dad, mum, two sisters and I travelled to London via Moscow on Aeroflot. I know there were many arguments with Pappa, my maternal grandfather, because he wanted Mum and us girls to stay in Dar es Salaam with him until Dad had found a job and somewhere to live. But my dad would not go without us all, so everything essential was shoved into one large suitcase and off we went. Having travelled with my girls as babies and toddlers I cannot even fathom how my parents got through that journey. Alien food on the plane, foreign faces and tongues, waiting for hours on end in queues and grey, soulless rooms.

But they did and we arrived at my first home in Tooting to live with Dad's brother-in-law – my Fua and his two children, Dino Bhai and Chanda Didi. I do remember this time. I remember the rooftop flat over a shop on Tooting Broadway. We were allowed to play out on the roof as long as we didn't go near the big hole which led to the lower courtyard. I remember the curtain in the living room behind which we all slept. I remember thinking Chanda Didi was the most beautiful woman I'd ever seen and Dino Bhai was the cleverest man on Earth. He brought me picture books and read to me. I already knew a little English because I had gone to an English-speaking nursery school in Dodoma but, now I was hearing the language everywhere, it made more sense and I found it fascinating. I remember Fua telling us stories and laughing a lot. But I also remember hushed voices as the adults talked about things I didn't really understand back then.

We then moved to a rented room in a Punjabi household in Southall: 43 Trinity Road. I remember different cooking smells. Onions. I think I went to school smelling of onions every day because the landlady cooked all her evening meals first thing in the morning and we weren't allowed to shower until the evening. I still find frying onions rather jarring though I love eating them. We had no visitors there. We got the bus to Tooting every weekend to see my Fua and his family.

After that we moved to Copley Close, a council estate in Hanwell. It was horrible. It stank of wee, the lights never worked and the bins were always full. But I loved that flat. It was enormous and I got my own room — with a desk and a bookshelf. The sitting room was huge and adjoined to the kitchen. This is where my food memories start. Mum worked in the former Gillette factory in Brentford and then she moved to a different place in Hammersmith. She would prep dinner before leaving for work in the early hours and leave snacks out for us to have for breakfast and after school. She'd bring home food her friends had made — Punjabi, Sri Lankan, South Indian, Caribbean — all the immigrant cultures that were starting to settle in London at the time.

We got a telephone and a car. Friends came to visit. We got Lego and dolls. Cousins came to stay with us and we went to stay with them. We made so much food. So many snacks for everyone to take home for the week — samosas and toasted sandwiches from leftovers; *bhakarvari* for treats; *ganthiya*; *dhokra*; *ondhwo* and *bhajia* for breakfasts. Each cousin had a different speciality and there were assembly lines like in the factories where Mum worked. The same cousins who held me, carried me and played with me back in Dodoma now taught me how to peel a potato, clean rice, pick out the bad lentils and beans and make *rotli*. Daksha, Mina, Saroj and Chandrika.

I realise now how central food was to every activity. Living in an alien environment you need something constant, something familiar. I was too young to be conscious of it at the time but later, when I went to university in Germany and France, it really hit me. I didn't see any foods there that I was familiar with and so I started cooking the ones I knew.

Back then, even though both my parents worked, we didn't have much money and the ingredients we used for Gujarati cooking must have been difficult to come by. Things were used sparingly but creatively to make a balanced and filling meal. Nothing was wasted and it was from these main meals that we snacked throughout the week.

Me in Tooting, 1976

My dad's persistence in retaking his banking qualifications on arrival in England paid off and he got a better job in the City. He and my mum bought a three-bedroom house in Perivale and we moved in around the time I started secondary school. Many relatives lived close by and it was a short bus ride to Ealing Road in Wembley which had become a Gujarati neighbourhood and shopping hub. The house had a garden and so when Baa came to stay she made *papad* which would dry in the sunny garden. Govind Bapa's wife, Bhabhu, would make *limbu pani* — sweet and salty lemonade made from fresh lemons like they did back in Rajkot —

and we'd sit on the doorstep outside doing our homework. Sashi Masi would do her *vaghars* (tempering) down at the bottom of the garden lest they would stink the house out. It had space in the kitchen for everyone to congregate before Diwali to make *fafra*, *sev* and *chevro*. And Mum would feed Beverley – the little girl next door – with hot *rotli* with ghee and jaggery. My parents still live in this house and, aside from paintwork and a fully paved back garden, it really hasn't changed much since then. My girls have toddled around the kitchen holding *rotli* just like Beverley did, slurping their orange milkshakes. I must have made over a thousand *rotli* in that house and received countless smacks round the head for eating too many of Mum's *dhokra* whilst they were cooling. Dad makes *masala chai* on the same cooker every day and the oven is still an extra store cupboard for the ghee and spices.

It was like Piccadilly Circus the whole time I was living there and then I moved away to university and beyond and realised how much I had taken it all for granted. When you first live by yourself in a tiny room with a shared kitchen, it's really hard to make the kind of food I grew up with. I only knew quantities for making portions for ten or twenty people so I started to experiment and adapt what I'd been taught to make enough just for me. Aside from sandwiches and pizza I had never really tasted any other cuisine. My Italian friends taught me how to make a very simple tomato sauce for pasta. For years I couldn't eat it as it was and appreciate the simple flavours of tomatoes and basil. It was a great midnight snack but I tempered it, added spices, and sometimes ate it with *rotli* (see *Vaghareli* Pasta on page 91).

Above: My Tone and me,
March 1997

Right: Amber Priya
and Amy Sienna, 2022

Attending university in Cologne, Germany gave me a love of bread. I'd never tasted anything other than Mother's Pride white sliced bread, and walking into a German bakery is still a Willy Wonka experience for me. Wholegrain rye bread with *dhal* is a game-changer and German seeded rolls make excellent sandwiches from leftover *shaak* or curry. France gave me a love of cheese, patisserie and desserts. *Rotli*, with creamy Brie and Lata Kaki's Red Pepper Chutney (page 142) for dipping is divine.

And Japan. Well, Japan gave me my Tone. Without him I would never have understood how to simplify a recipe or have tried a whole host of different foods. I never liked eggs, for example, but every Sunday in our little communal kitchen Tone would make Spanish tortilla, presenting it with a flourish and an '*olé!*' These came to be known as Tone's Potato Lovelies because they were genuinely a lovely way to eat eggs. Without him I would never have been brave enough to try even simple Japanese food like maki rolls (even though now I pimp them up with carrot *sambharo* or *lasan ni* chutney). I found a life partner to travel the world with and have my babies with. Amber Priya and Amy Sienna have grown up on traditional Gujarati food as well as dishes from around the world and we have personalised them along the way. They love baked beans so we added potatoes and turned it into *shaak* when they were little and just discovering spice. Today that's still our meal of choice after a holiday.

As a family we travel a lot, planning trips just so we can eat specific foods from specific towns, bringing home some ingredients we'd never even heard of. 'Mumma, can you make that cake we had in Paris?' or 'Dadda, can we have those sardines like in Essaouria?' Living and travelling together has brought a whole new set of ingredients and dishes into my traditional Gujarati kitchen.

Our food today is a cultural mishmash of what we like from around the world. But every now and then I find myself feeding my girls the same dishes I used to eat or making them because they had them at Nanni's house. When they're sick or not feeling great or have just had a bad day, I'll resort back to *ghee ne bhaath* – simply boiled basmati rice with salt and ghee – to make them feel better. It used to comfort me after school, and that feeling of comfort is embedded as much in the food itself as in the memory. It continues to remind me of where I've come from. The journey to who I am today.

A Word About Cousins, Aunties and Uncles

Mum is one of eight children and Dad is one of five. I have over twenty first cousins and many of them now have their own children and grandchildren. That's just my directly related family!

Everyone is an auntie or an uncle until you figure out how you are related, and then ideally you use the correct denomination and their name depending on which side of the family they are on. So, here's a quick summary:

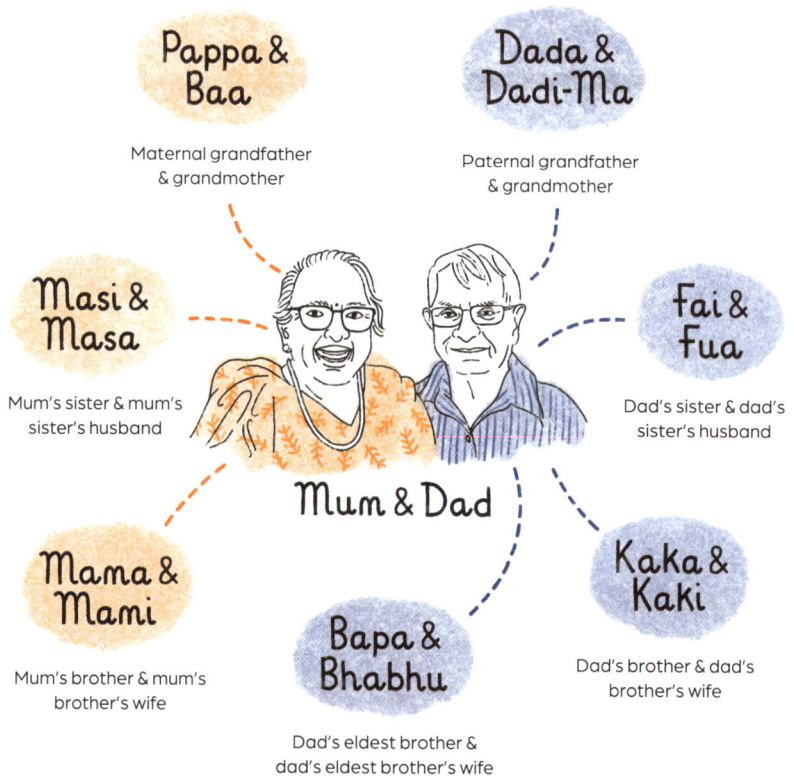

Pappa & Baa
Maternal grandfather & grandmother

Dada & Dadi-Ma
Paternal grandfather & grandmother

Masi & Masa
Mum's sister & mum's sister's husband

Fai & Fua
Dad's sister & dad's sister's husband

Mum & Dad

Mama & Mami
Mum's brother & mum's brother's wife

Kaka & Kaki
Dad's brother & dad's brother's wife

Bapa & Bhabhu
Dad's eldest brother & dad's eldest brother's wife

There are also special denominations for the ranking in the family; for example, the eldest brother's wife is *Jethani* and younger brother's wife, *Derani*. When I was younger, it was all a bit much to try and remember names and relations so we used to give everyone nicknames based on their attributes. My Daya Mami, for example: I think she is my mum's cousin on her father's side, hence my mum's 'sister' or Daya Mami. But I was never sure when I was little so I called her Socks Auntie because she always wore socks under her saree. My Sushila Auntie is another example. I never remember how we are related to her but I know it's very, very distant. My husband asked me once and I didn't remember so he just called her Across-the-Road Auntie and it's stuck. My girls called her the same as they were growing up.

We include first and second cousins as close family and I cannot even begin to count how many of them there are. It has to be over three hundred. A boy cousin is *Bhai* and a female cousin is *Ben*. An older female cousin is *Didi*.

You'll hear these denominations throughout the book.

About This Book

It is customary to offer refreshments when someone visits your home or to bring food when you are the visitor. It could be a full-scale meal, but if someone is just popping over then it is usually *katak batak*. This is slang for small bites, snacks, pre-food, a little something or other. *Katak* means 'a small piece' and *batak* means 'bite'. It sometimes gets shortened to *kut-but* with the verb 'do'. So, '*Chalo katak batak kare*' literally means 'let's do small bites'.

So why isn't this book called *Katak Batak*? Well, that would indeed have been a good name. Except in my family, it's called Biting Biting. Sometimes shortened to Biting with the 'i' drawn out a little. Biiiting.

There are some base recipes we commonly cook as meals and then often use to make Biting Biting. I've given you some variations and ideas but please do experiment with flavours and ingredients you like.

You'll find a summary of what's in my masala *dablo* (tin), store cupboards, fridge and freezer. This is not exhaustive but hopefully it gives you an idea of which ingredients you might like to buy. Gujarati food is very simple. Of all the regions in India I think we use the least complex variations of spices. If you are an experienced cook familiar with Indian food, you may find it quite plain so feel free to add more or less of what you like.

Mostly the recipes are Gujarati but every now and then you will find one that isn't because it's a favourite in our house and I wanted to share it with you.

My Masala *Dablo* (or Spice Tin)

Many people tell me that they are wary of cooking Indian food because of all the different spices. Gujarati food is very simple. If you invest in nothing else, invest in these key spices and you will be able to make a flavourful vegetarian meal.

You can buy them all in most supermarkets now, and online. One of my favourite places to buy online is Spice Kitchen, a lovely family-run business. They specialise in spice tins which come beautifully wrapped in sarees.

Chilli Powder (*Murchu*) There are so many different types of chillies and chilli powders. I use a medium-heat chilli powder and that's what the measures in this book are based on. Increase or decrease the quantity depending on your tastebuds and tolerance.

Cinnamon (*Taj*) I usually have a few sticks of cassia bark. It comes in randomly sized chunks and has a slightly stronger flavour than the perfectly sized cinnamon sticks you see in supermarkets.

Cloves (*Laving*) I use these sparingly because the flavour can be overpowering. The cloves always seem to end up in my husband's portion when my mum serves *dhal* and we tell him it's because we are all giving him some 'loving'.

Coriander (*Dhanna*) Ground coriander is a staple. I make it by lightly toasting coriander seeds and then grinding them to a fine powder in a spice blender. It doesn't take very long to do and I think it's a fresher taste. Plus your kitchen will smell amazing.

Cumin (*Jeera*) The most common type used in Gujarati food are the brown cumin seeds. I make my own ground cumin by toasting the seeds lightly and grinding them to a fine powder in a spice blender.

Mustard Seeds (*Rai*) I use the tiny dark brown/black whole mustard seeds for cooking. They will fizzle and pop in hot oil to release their flavour.

Salt (*Nimak*) I use finely ground sea salt or table salt.

Turmeric (*Hardar*) Powdered turmeric is a vibrant yellow colour. It has an earthy flavour and many anti-inflammatory properties. Try not to get it on your fingers as it will stain. Unless of course you have a cut in which case feel free to do what my mum does and stick your finger in. She says it seals the wound and keeps infections at bay.

In My Store Cupboard

I have a wide range of other spices, condiments, beans, pulses and flours in my store cupboard, and can spend hours in the world food aisle at the supermarket to see what else I can buy. These are the things I use most frequently.

Ajowan These tiny seeds look a bit like celery seeds. We use them in many dishes to help with digestion – Mum always used to give them to us soaked in warm water when we had a bloaty tummy. They are sometimes called carom seeds.

Almonds Flaked, whole and ground. Useful for making desserts and also garnishes.

Amchur A zesty flavoured powder made from unripe green mangoes. It gives a citrus kick when sprinkled on *bhajia*, yoghurt or salads.

Cashew Nuts I get the unroasted, whole cashews to cook with, and a jar of toasted ones for toppings.

Chapatti Flour This is a special type of wheat flour used for making *rotli* and *parotha*. I buy the fine wholewheat version called *asli atta*.

Chevro Otherwise known as Bombay Mix. This is readily available in supermarkets but I suggest you seek out an Indian specialist and taste some of the different varieties on offer. You can buy sweet versions and super fiery versions. Even versions with cornflakes!

Chilli Oil Super handy for quick drizzles to give a fiery heat. You can mix up your own version using three tablespoons of rapeseed or olive oil to one teaspoon of chilli flakes and one teaspoon chilli powder.

Coconut Milk Tins of coconut milk are much easier to store than the cartons so I bulk buy them. Shake well before use and don't forget to use the thick bit that is stuck to the lid!

Desiccated Coconut A great substitute for fresh coconut. Simply hydrate it by leaving it for ten minutes in boiling water and then draining through a sieve. It will then be nice and fluffy.

Eno Fruit Salts We use Eno as a raising agent. I've tried using baking powder or bicarbonate instead but I don't get the same results. You should be able to buy it in most chemists if you don't live near an Indian grocer.

Ganthiya Thick gram flour style noodles which are brilliant snacks on their own with tea or can be added for crunch to *dhal*. Worth keeping a jar handy as they are also great in tomato and onion *shaak*.

Garam Masala Literally translated this means 'hot spice blend' and each household will have its own recipe. I don't use garam masala very often so I buy it in small quantities.

Garlic I grow my own garlic and always have some handy. Many of my mum's family don't eat garlic because it is said to have a sedative effect on the body. Dad's side don't like it in dishes but swear by a daily spoonful of garlic-packed *lasan ni* chutney on the side of dinner. I must take after his side of the family because I love it!

Ghee This is clarified butter and it sits proudly on my kitchen counter because I am a *ghee* fanatic. I use it as a drizzle on *dhal*, liberally basted onto *rotli* or *parotha* and in many of the sweet dishes in this book. You can make your own by very gently simmering regular butter until all the impurities have bubbled to the surface where you can scoop them off. The rest sink to the bottom of the pan and taste delicious! I like to spread them generously on toast with some brown sugar. If you're buying it, get the best organic version that you can afford. I like Happy Butter Ghee or Ghee Easy brands.

Gram Flour Made from ground chickpeas, this pale yellow flour has a nutty flavour. We use it for sweet and savoury dishes so I always have some handy. Sometimes called besan or chickpea flour.

Jaggery I could eat jaggery all day long. It is made from unrefined cane sugar and has an earthy sweetness. If you struggle to find it, use soft dark brown sugar instead.

Maize Flour Essential for making *ugali* when craving a taste of Tanzania. Buy the white variety.

Pawa Dried, flattened parboiled rice flakes available in different thicknesses. I use the medium variety.

Peanuts I always buy plain untoasted, skinned peanuts.

Red Lentils Mum makes *dhal* with *toor dhal* which is oily and chunky. I don't have the patience for the soaking and preparation this takes so I use basic split red lentils.

Rice I buy basmati rice. Mostly white but increasingly brown too.

Rice Flour Essential for *Kichee* (page 73), one of my favourite dishes in this book.

Rose Syrup Essential for making *Falooda* (page 172) or stirring into Karamsi's *Seero* (page 160). It keeps for ages.

Seeds Sunflower, sesame and pumpkin seeds are my staples. I toast them up in small batches and keep them in jars on the kitchen counter so they are always to hand as a topping or garnish.

Semolina This is a pale yellow/beige flour made from durum wheat. I buy the coarse semolina. Note that this isn't the same as either polenta (which is made from corn) or yellow wheat flour.

Sev Fried gram flour vermicelli-style noodles, often used as a topping. I like them sprinkled on to *masala chai* and slurped up using a spoon. It's a Gujarati equivalent of dipping biscuits in tea!

Split Mustard Seeds I use these for pickles. They keep for ages so a small packet is fine.

Tins I bulk buy tins from the Asian grocery store. Chickpeas, kidney beans, black-eyed beans, baked beans, San Marzano tomatoes and coconut milk tins are always in my trolley.

In My Fridge

I have a very small, under the counter fridge. This really does help me waste less food. When we had a big fridge, I kept finding things at the bottom or the back which never got used and ended up throwing them away. These are the staples I almost always have inside.

Coriander I wish I could grow this herb as I use so much of it but, alas, I have never been able to. I tend to buy a couple of bunches from the market every week and store them on a damp paper towel in a sealed food bag. Or in cooler months you can just pop the bunch in a glass of water on the counter.

Cheese Every possible kind. I love cheese. We are never without Cheddar or Brie.

Curry Leaves Don't buy dried ones as they really don't have the same flavour or smell. Seek out fresh ones, take them off the stalk and store them on damp kitchen tissue in a tightly sealed container in the fridge. They should keep quite well for a few weeks. Careful when you add them to oil because if they are wet then they may cause the oil to spit.

Ginger I always have a clump of ginger in the fridge. I also make up grated ginger in oil in small batches so it's fast to use. Simply grate a clump of ginger, pop it in a sterilised jar and cover with sunflower or rapeseed oil.

Green Chillies A handful of fresh green chillies goes into the weekly shop. I finely chop or blitz them in the food processor and then store them in a sterilised jar covered with a thin layer of sunflower or rapeseed oil. I find that this way you get a more consistent heat without having to figure out which ones are hotter than others and how many to use.

Tamarind A rich sweet and sour paste made from tamarind pulp. I find the ready-made paste more convenient than the block of pulp which you have to soak before use. It keeps for ages.

Yoghurt Mum used to make yoghurt every day. It's more a mellow curd than yoghurt – the consistency of silken tofu. I like eating yoghurt on its own rather than in cooking so I buy thick Greek yoghurt or skyr.

My Essential Ingredients

In My Freezer

My freezer is also very small but the must haves are noted below.

Cassava I grew up calling this *mogo* as that's what it's called in Tanzania where it is a staple. It is a starchy root vegetable with thick brown skin and a stringy white flesh. I buy the frozen chunks or chips which have been boiled before freezing. I cook them from frozen and they defrost as they cook.

Coconut If you find fresh coconut, buy it and keep it in your freezer where it will keep for months. To prepare it for freezing, let the flesh dry out for a day and then grate half coarsely and half finely. Mix together and pop into a freezer bag. It breaks up more easily in a bag than a container.

Mung Beans These are such a staple at home and I love them so much that I batch boil them 'til they are just tender and keep them in my freezer. You can use them right from frozen and the cooking will turn them creamy and soft.

Sprouted Mung Beans If you have never had a go at sprouting, mung beans are a great place to start. Wash them well and soak them for a few hours. Rinse and then leave them on a damp tea towel unbothered for a few days. You'll see sprouts forming. You can then gather them up and freeze them. Add them to *Vagharela Bhaath* (page 112) or *Pawa Bateta* (page 115).

Peas One of the best vegetables to have in the freezer as you can turn them into so many tasty dishes quickly.

Spinach I like the frozen chopped spinach rather than the leaves. It is an easy way to get veggies into *dhal* or *shaak*.

Sweetcorn As with peas, there are so many things you can do with corn. I always have some kernels which I prefer frozen rather than in tins. But I also love sweetcorn on the cob, which you can also get frozen in bags, cut into bite-sized chunks.

FEVER-TREE
Refreshingly Light
"MEDITERRANEAN"
TONIC WATER

CIRIO
1856
SUPERCIRIO
Doppio
Concentrato
Double Concentrated
tomato purée
Tomato Paste
Double Concentré
de Tomates
100% POMODORO
ITALIANO

CIRIO
1856
SUPERCIRIO
Doppio
Concentrato
Double Concentrated
tomato purée
Tomato Paste
Double Concentré
de Tomates
100% POMODORO
ITALIANO

CAKE DECORATING
Red or D

ORGANIC
ORGANIC Wholemeal Buckwheat Flour

GRAM FLOUR
100% PURE

BEER SNACKS

My dad is not much of a drinker. I've only ever seen him drink beer – in the tiniest of cans, the ones you get on planes. He never went to the pub or a bar as far as I am aware, and we didn't really eat in restaurants 'til I was in my twenties, and even then he rarely came let alone had a drink. My English husband Tone, on the other hand, is a very social drinker. He loves a beer or two. A memory that always makes me laugh is the first time my husband – then fiancé – came to visit me at my parental home and Dad asked if he wanted a beer. Of course, my husband said yes and out came the little tins – which my husband necked in one go like a shot, not realising he was supposed to sip them. Funnier still was the snack that accompanied the beer: cubes of cheese sprinkled over with a little chilli powder and cumin. Left to his own devices this is what my dad would snack on. Thankfully Gujarati women are the best at creating little nibbles to have with beer. Note – I'm not a fan of beer and can attest that all of these snacks work well with a glass of wine too.

POPPADOMS

Masala Papad

There are three ways to cook a *papad*:

1. Heat a little oil in a shallow frying pan. When it reaches about 180°C, gently place in the *papad* which should fluff up. Use tongs to keep it as flat as you can, as it will naturally curl up.
2. Take a pair of metal tongs and use them to toast your *papad* over an open flame. Hold it over the flame for a few seconds, working your way around until all the raw bits are puffed up and evenly toasted, and then flip it to cook the other side.
3. Brush a little water on to both sides of the *papad* and microwave in 20 second bursts. Turn over each time so it's evenly cooked.

Whichever way you choose, the best way to eat these is laden with masala toppings.

These toppings make enough each to sprinkle lightly over two 15cm *papads*. Allow two *papads* per person.

Tomato First make some pink pickled onion. Slice a small red onion and put in a bowl covered with boiling water for ten minutes. Drain and then toss through the juice of half a lemon and a teaspoon of salt.

Take one large tomato and chop it into 1cm cubes. Add half a teaspoon salt, half a teaspoon chilli powder, half a teaspoon ground cumin and two tablespoons of freshly chopped coriander. Sprinkle this over the cooked *papad* and then add a few slices of the pink pickled onion.

Sweetcorn To a cup of cooked sweetcorn add the juice of half a lemon, half a teaspoon of salt, half a teaspoon ground cumin, a teaspoon of finely chopped green chillies, half of a small chopped onion, a tablespoon of sesame seeds and a couple of tablespoons of chopped fresh coriander. Toss it all together and then sprinkle over your cooked *papad*.

Capsicum Finely chop a small green capsicum and half an onion. Add two tablespoons of Green Chilli and Coriander Chutney (see page 151), two tablespoons of chopped fresh coriander and two to three tablespoons of crushed roasted peanuts. Toss it all together and sprinkle over your cooked *papad*. You can make a red version using a red capsicum and Lata Kaki's Red Pepper Chutney (page 150).

Street sellers all over Gujarat sell these lovely spicy pastries, each with their own unique recipes depending on the town. Traditionally they are made with gram flour and fried rather than baked. Some aunties make them sweeter by adding more sugar or jaggery, others add poppy seeds and omit the fennel. Use this recipe as a base and experiment to find the combination you like the most.

Makes 12–15

100g desiccated coconut
4 tbsp sesame seeds
2 tsp fennel seeds
2 tsp chilli powder
2 tsp ground coriander
2 tsp ground cumin
2 tsp amchur
2 tsp salt
4 tbsp granulated sugar
1 sheet ready-rolled puff pastry
2–3 tbsp tamarind paste
    or lemon juice

Lightly toast the coconut, sesame and fennel seeds in a dry frying pan – you only want to release the flavours so toast until they *just* start to brown. Leave to cool slightly and then blitz in a spice grinder or food processor 'til you get a coarse, sandy mixture. Add the chilli powder, ground coriander, ground cumin, amchur, salt and sugar and whisk to combine well.

Preheat the oven to 200°C (180°C fan). Line a baking tray with greaseproof paper.

Lay out the ready-rolled puff pastry sheet and brush the tamarind paste or lemon juice all the way to the edges. Now evenly sprinkle over the spice mix so you have a layer about the same thickness all over. Push the mixture into the pastry gently with the back of a spoon.

Roll the pastry up along the long edge and then stick the end down with a little water to stop it unfolding while it bakes. You should have a nice long cigar shape – a bit like a thin Swiss roll. Cut it into slices about a centimetre thick and place them onto the prepared baking sheet leaving a bit of space in between. Bake for 20–30 minutes until they are just starting to brown.

Tips

To make sure the spice mix is evenly pushed into the pastry, instead of using a spoon you can cover it with a sheet of greaseproof paper and gently roll over the paper with a rolling pin. Remove the paper and roll up as above.

I use thread to cut the slices evenly. Take about 20cm of plain sewing thread, place it under your rolled up pastry and then bring either end of the thread up and over the pastry to cut it.

Serving Suggestions

I also like these dipped into plain yoghurt for elevenses.

They make a good *chaat* crushed over a bowl of yoghurt, then topped with chopped tomatoes and a drizzle of any of the chutneys in 'Chutneys and Pickles' on page 140.

Some of the aunties mix the spice mix with mashed potato for a more substantial filling.

MIXED SPICED NUTS

When I was in Marrakech I loved the nut bazaar. Every single kind of nut imaginable, available in any quantity you wanted. What's more, they'd knock up a batch of flavoured nuts with your personal combination of spices before you could even get some money out to pay. These nuts always remind me of that bazaar, and the kitchen almost smells as good when I make them.

Serves 4

50g whole almonds
50g cashews
50g peanuts
50g hazelnuts
50g walnut halves
1 egg white
2 tsp ground cumin
2 tsp ground coriander
¼ tsp cinnamon
1 tsp salt
sea salt for sprinkling
garlic powder (optional)

Preheat the oven to 170°C (150°C fan) and line a baking tray with greaseproof paper. Spread the nuts over the paper and bake for ten minutes.

In a small bowl, whisk the egg white 'til frothy and then toss in the nuts making sure they are evenly coated. Sprinkle over the cumin, coriander, cinnamon and salt and then mix again before returning to the oven for 15 minutes until the nuts are slightly browned.

As soon as they come out of the oven, sprinkle over a little sea salt and garlic powder. Leave to cool before eating. Ideally make these on the day you will eat them but they will store OK in an airtight container for a few days if you have leftovers.

This recipe is inspired by peanut brittle but takes a little less time and effort to make.

Serves 4

350g raw unsalted peanuts
175g runny honey
2 tbsp chilli powder
sea salt for sprinkling

vegetable oil for greasing

Preheat the oven to 170°C (150°C fan). Grease a baking tray lightly with oil.

Combine the peanuts and honey in a pan and pop onto a low heat for about five minutes 'til the honey is warm. Add the chilli powder and stir through.

Spread the mixture over the greased baking tray and bake for 15–20 minutes. The nuts should be a golden brown. Take them out of the oven and loosen the peanuts from the tray. Leave to cool completely and then break into pieces for serving.

CHILLI AND HONEY ROASTED PEANUTS

SPICY STIR-FRIED CASHEWS

Vagharela Kaju

I love cashews. I could eat them any which way they come but I particularly like these with a cold Mexican or Spanish beer. You need to make them and eat them rather than make them and store them as they are best eaten on the same day.

Serves 4

3 tbsp sunflower or rapeseed oil
1 tbsp mustard seeds
1 tbsp cumin seeds
5–6 curry leaves
200g raw unsalted cashew nuts
1 tsp salt
2 tsp chilli powder
2 tsp ground cumin

Heat the oil in a wok for a few minutes on a medium heat. Add the mustard and cumin seeds and the curry leaves and let them fizzle and pop for a few seconds. Stir in the cashew nuts and sauté for a few minutes 'til the cashews start turning brown. Turn the heat off and then add the salt, chilli powder and ground cumin. Stir well to combine the spices evenly.

These are really lovely warm, right out of the wok.

During the summer holidays Across-the-Road Auntie used to take us to visit her mum who lived on a rough council estate in Edmonton. It was really exciting because we'd take the bus and she'd let us sit upstairs right at the front. Her mum lived on the top floor of a tower block but I never saw the rundown council estate for what it was. To me it was one of the most breathtaking places ever because I could see far out across London. We would often stay over and she'd make us cheese on toast this way for breakfast. It's stuck with me and I've made it like this ever since. Try it. So crisp and worth the effort.

CUMIN-SPICED CHEESE ON TOAST

Serves 2

butter – salted or unsalted is fine
2 slices thick, sliced white bread
150g Cheddar cheese, grated
   (use more or less as you wish)
ground cumin for sprinkling
chilli powder (optional)

Butter one side of each slice of bread and pop them – buttered-side up – under the grill to toast 'til golden brown.

Take them out and evenly distribute the Cheddar cheese over the top of the non-buttered side. Return to the grill for a few minutes until the cheese is just starting to bubble. Sprinkle over the ground cumin and cut into posh triangles. If you want heat as well as spice, sprinkle on some chilli powder.

GRAM FLOUR CRACKERS WITH FRIED GREEN CHILLIES

Patta Ganthiya

When I lived at home, making snacks for Diwali was a big event. We would congregate at someone's house to cook the snacks in batches. My sisters, cousins and I would be given various jobs to do on the assembly line. Mine was rolling any form of dough because I can roll it very thinly. Nowadays we mostly buy Diwali snacks because everyone's lives seem that much busier than they were. But every now and then I make these crackers in small batches as my husband loves them.

Serves 4

150g gram flour
¼ tsp bicarbonate of soda
¼ tsp coarsely ground black pepper
¼ tsp ajowan seeds
½ tsp salt
1 tbsp sunflower oil plus more
    for kneading
10–15 green chillies, slit lengthways
    with seeds removed
salt for sprinkling

vegetable oil for deep frying

Mix the gram flour, bicarb, black pepper, ajowan seeds and salt together and then rub in the oil. Add just-boiled water a little at a time until you can bring the mixture into a firm dough. It doesn't matter if it is sticky but it shouldn't be too soft; otherwise it will be hard to roll.

Pour a little oil onto your hands and then knead the dough for about five minutes until it is smooth and doesn't feel as sticky. Divide the dough into 12–15 balls and then shape each ball into a short sausage. Lightly oil your work surface and roll each sausage out 'til it's just a few millimetres thick.

Heat about 5cm of oil in a deep-sided pan to 180°C and then gently lower in one of the pieces of thinly rolled dough. I fry the crackers one by one for a few minutes on each side. They will harden as they fry and sometimes they curl up but they shouldn't turn brown. Drain on kitchen paper and sprinkle over a pinch of salt. They will crisp up as they cool.

Once you are done frying the crackers, you can fry the green chillies. Make sure they are completely dry and you have a splatter guard because they can pop right at you! Drop all the chillies into the hot oil 'til they blister – this should take only a few seconds. Take them out immediately with a slotted spoon and drain on kitchen paper. Sprinkle over salt and that's it! Serve them on the side of the crackers.

Gajjar No Sambharo
MATCHSTICK CARROT SALAD

When I was in my teens we went on our first family holiday back to India. My father wanted us to take the overnight train from Mumbai to Rajkot. He made a huge fuss of making sure we sat in a specific carriage. I'd never seen him elbow people out of the way before but he made sure we all sat on the left-hand side of the train. All became clear when the train pulled up at Ahmedabad station the following morning and our carriage stopped right in front of the best breakfast stall on the platform. We ate this warm carrot salad out of a newspaper cone with fried green chillies, *patta ganthiya* and hot spicy tea. It was the best breakfast I'd ever had, but I've since discovered it also tastes insanely good with beer or crisp white wine.

Serves 2–4

3 tbsp vegetable oil
1 heaped tsp small black
  mustard seeds
4 green chillies, thinly sliced
  lengthways into strips
200g carrots, julienned or
  cut into matchsticks
juice of 1 lemon
½ tsp turmeric
1 tsp salt

Heat the oil in a pan on a medium heat for a few minutes; check the oil is hot enough by dropping in a mustard seed – it should fizzle and pop. Add the rest of the mustard seeds and green chillies, closely followed by the carrots. Reduce the heat to low and then stir in the lemon juice, turmeric and salt. Cover and leave to simmer gently for ten minutes until the carrots are *just* tender.

Serve with *Patta Ganthiya* (page 38). I also like it mixed into plain rice or rolled into a wrap with leftover *rotli*. A classic fusion from my time in Japan is using this as a filling when we make Japanese cucumber maki rolls. It sounds so weird but really works!

SPICED MUNG BEANS

Vagharela Mug

After a wedding it is customary to invite the new couple to your home for a meal. With the size of my family it took about six months to get round everyone in the UK. Recognising that many of the family had been a little frosty about a mixed-race marriage, one of the first to welcome us to his home was Girdharlal Fua. Over the years he always, always came over and chatted with my husband at events lest he felt lonely. This recipe is dedicated to him and his kindness. His son Viraj tells me this was one of his favourite snacks. It's incredibly moreish and works well as a salad or *dhal* topping too.

Serves 2–4

150g whole mung beans,
    soaked overnight and drained
2 tbsp sunflower or rapeseed oil
½ tsp ground cumin
½ tsp garlic powder
½ tsp garam masala
½ tsp chilli powder
1 tsp salt
juice of half a lemon to serve

Preheat the oven to 180°C (160°C fan) and line a baking tray with greaseproof paper.

Dry fry the soaked mung beans in a large, flat frying pan to remove some of the residual water. Add the oil and toss together well. The mung beans should now be nicely coated. Add the cumin, garlic powder, garam masala, chilli powder and salt and toss together again before spreading out on the lined baking tray.

Bake for 15–20 minutes until the mung beans have crisped up. Serve hot or cold with a squeeze of lemon juice. These are easy to store in an airtight container and keep for a couple of weeks.

Nobody used the oven in our house. It was an extra cupboard for storing the masala tin, *rotli* pan and ghee. One day we got a free cookbook from the milkman. It had all the classic recipes in it like scones, fairy cakes and chocolate cookies. There was a recipe in there for sugary wafers and I decided to have a go. I've been playing with them ever since. They don't take long to make and are super tasty with *chai* and have often gotten an 'ooooh' from the aunties.

Makes 20–25

80g plain flour plus more
    for kneading
30ml rapeseed oil
30ml beer
30g granulated sugar
1 tbsp sesame seeds
1 tbsp fennel seeds
sea salt

4cm biscuit cutter
blowtorch (optional)

Put the flour in a bowl, add a pinch of salt and then gently mix in the oil and beer. It should come together into a rough dough. Pop this out onto a floured surface and knead it lightly for about five minutes 'til it is smooth and elastic. Cover and set aside in the fridge for 15 minutes.

While the dough is resting, preheat the oven to 200°C (180°C fan) and line a couple of baking trays with greaseproof paper. In a bowl, mix the sugar with the sesame and fennel seeds and set aside.

Roll the dough out between two sheets of greaseproof paper to about 5mm thick. Cut out discs using the biscuit cutter and place these one by one onto the lined baking trays. Gather up the dough scraps and repeat until you've used it all up.

Brush the discs with a little water and then sprinkle over the sugar and seeds mixture, patting it down gently so it sticks to the dough. Bake for eight minutes. Once the wafers are out of the oven, lightly blowtorch them to melt the sugar a bit more and then leave them to cool completely. If you don't have a blowtorch you can simply pop them under a medium-hot grill. These are best eaten warm and work well with tea as well as beer.

FENNEL AND SESAME WAFERS

My friend Pradeep is an exceptional cook. He was born in Kenya and we share a love of East African ingredients; cassava is one of our favourites. You can buy it fresh in most Asian or Greek supermarkets but I buy the pre-cooked frozen version and use it right from the freezer.

As teenagers we were both part of the Youth Committee of The Shri Vishwakarma Association, a community of families from Gujarat and East Africa descended from the Suthar caste who were carpenters by trade. We volunteered most weekends organising Gujarati classes, pantomimes, discos and boat parties. I have very fond memories of those years and made some everlasting friendships. After many a late-night event we would end up in one of two places: Scratchwood Services on the M1 for beans on toast and tea or Pradeep's house for *mari mogo* and a few more beers.

Serves 4–6

500g frozen cooked cassava (*mogo*) chips or 2-inch chunks
4 tbsp sunflower or rapeseed oil
4 whole green chillies, roughly sliced
5–6 curry leaves
2 tsp salt
2 tsp coarsely ground black pepper
juice of half a lemon
3 tbsp chopped fresh coriander

Bring a pan of water to the boil and cook the mogo for five minutes to soften, then drain. Heat the oil in a large wok over a medium flame and then add the green chillies and curry leaves. This might make you cough so have the lid and a glass of water handy!

Add the cooked cassava chips or chunks, salt and pepper and give it a good stir so the cassava is coated well. Turn the heat to low and then put the lid on and cook for five minutes. Toss the cassava around and then put the lid back on and cook for another five minutes. The cassava should be nice and crisp in places. If not, then repeat one more time.

Add the lemon juice and fresh coriander and serve hot.

Serving Suggestions

We used to huddle around the pan and just pick at this with our fingers.

It's lovely served with yoghurt or Green Chilli and Coriander Chutney (page 151) as a dip.

I also like making a *chaat* from this. Put a layer of *mari mogo* on a flat plate, and then spoon over some plain yoghurt. Sprinkle with salt-and-pepper crisps (I like to use matchstick crisps) or crushed *papads*. Then add a little more fresh coriander and it's ready to eat.

Variation

Spicy Tomato *Mogo* Pradeep has a huge spice cupboard and is a dabbler when he cooks. There's always a little bit of this and a tiny bit of that so no two batches are ever the same. Here is what I wrote down the last time I visited and watched him cook a tomato-based variation. It was lovely with a glass of Malbec which his wife, Hina, is very partial to.

Toss 500g cassava in 4 tbsp sunflower or rapeseed oil. Then add 2 tsp salt, 2 tbsp soy sauce, 2 crushed cloves of garlic, ½ tsp turmeric, ½ tsp ground coriander, ½ tsp ground cumin, 2 tsp dried *kasturi methi*, 1 tsp *deggi mirch* or chilli powder and 150g passata.

Mix it all together and then bake in a 200°C (180°C fan) oven for 20 minutes, stirring halfway through.

BHAJIA

Bhajia are an essential part of Biting Biting. No matter what the occasion and regardless of the guest, there is always some *bhajia* action on the table.

I use a mini deep fryer but you can easily use a saucepan. Just make sure you have enough oil in the pan so the *bhajia* can freely float without sticking to the bottom. Depending on the size of your pan go with around 8—10cm deep.

Bhajia are best eaten as soon as they are made. However if you do have leftovers they are excellent as *chaat*. Just layer the *bhajia* on a platter, spoon over Greek yoghurt, then sprinkle on a bit of *sev* or even *chevro*, some chopped tomatoes and finely chopped fresh herbs.

ONION FRITTERS

Dhoonghree na Bhajia

Serves 6–8

3–4 large white onions
200g gram flour
50g rice flour
1½ tsp salt
2 tsp ajowan seeds
1 tsp chilli powder (optional)
juice of 1 large lemon
4 tbsp chopped fresh coriander
amchur for sprinkling

vegetable oil, for frying

Finely slice the onions and set aside. Mix the gram flour, rice flour, salt, ajowan seeds and chilli powder together in a bowl. Add the lemon juice and around 200–250ml warm water and mix well so there are no lumps – you need a thick pouring consistency like custard. Add the coriander and sliced onions and toss them together in the batter.

In a deep fat fryer or deep-sided pan, heat 8–10cm vegetable oil to 180°C. Take a spoonful of the *bhajia* mixture and drop it gently into the oil. Fry two to three at a time, for about five minutes, turning halfway through. (If you overcrowd the fryer or pan then they will all stick together and you will reduce the heat of the oil, making the *bhajia* greasy rather than crisp.) Drain on kitchen paper and sprinkle with some amchur before eating.

Variations

You can experiment with the spices in this recipe. Sometimes I use coarse black pepper instead of the chilli powder and replace the ajowan seeds with fennel, cumin or even lightly crushed coriander seeds.

You can add julienned carrots or courgettes, shredded cabbage or spinach, or chunks of broccoli (or all of these!) to the onions. *Bhajia* are a great way of using up odds and ends of vegetables at the end of the week.

Serves 6–8

200g gram flour
50g rice flour
1½ tsp salt
2 tsp cumin seeds
1 tsp chilli powder (optional)
juice of 1 large lemon
4 tbsp chopped fresh coriander
350g Cheddar cheese, cut into
   3cm chunks
250g baby spinach, roughly chopped

vegetable oil, for frying

Whisk the gram and rice flours together in a bowl and then add the salt, cumin seeds and chilli powder (if you're using it). Add the lemon juice and 200ml warm water and mix well so there are no lumps. Stir in the coriander, cheese and spinach and mix so everything is coated well in the batter.

In a deep fat fryer or deep-sided pan, heat 8–10cm vegetable oil to 180°C. Take a spoonful of the *bhajia* mixture and drop it gently into the hot oil. Cook for about five minutes turning halfway through. Fry two to three at a time: if you overcrowd the fryer or pan then they will all stick together and you will reduce the heat of the oil, making the *bhajia* greasy rather than crisp. Drain on kitchen paper and eat as they are or with chutney of your choice.

Lobia na Bhajia
BLACK-EYED BEANS BHAJIA

When I was travelling in South India with my husband, one of my favourite breakfasts was *mehdu vadas* – savoury ring doughnuts made from *urad dhal*, spiced simply with green chillies and ginger. At home I often crave these, forgetting that the *urad dhal* needs soaking for a few hours. So instead I make this very distantly related version using tinned, cooked black-eyed beans. They are the perfect vessel for scooping up chutneys.

Serves 2–4

1 × 400g tin of black-eyed beans, drained
2 tsp finely chopped green chillies
2 tsp grated ginger
2 tsp grated garlic (optional)
1 tsp cumin seeds
1 tsp salt
¼ tsp bicarbonate of soda

vegetable oil for frying

Blitz all the ingredients together in a mixer. There should be enough moisture from the beans to make a thick batter but, if not, you can add a few tablespoons of water so you get a thick, hummus-like consistency.

In a deep fat fryer or deep-sided pan, heat 8–10cm vegetable oil to 180°C. When it's ready, gently dollop heaped teaspoonfuls of the mixture into the oil and fry for about five minutes, turning gently so the *bhajia* cook evenly, until they are golden brown. Drain on kitchen paper and eat immediately with chutneys of your choice.

Serving Suggestions

I like these with a squeeze of fresh lemon juice and some plain yoghurt or Coconut and Yoghurt Chutney (page 150) for a simple breakfast.

Leftover *bhajia* make quite nice dumplings in tomato sauce. Put the contents of a 400g tin of chopped tomatoes into a pan and stir in a teaspoon of salt and a teaspoon of chilli powder. Place on a gentle heat to warm through. Heat two tablespoons of oil in a small frying pan and add a teaspoon of mustard seeds and a few curry leaves. Pour this over the tomatoes, stir and then simmer gently for five minutes, dropping the *bhajia* in to warm through right at the end. Eat warm, garnished with fresh coriander, toasted sunflower or pumpkin seeds and a dollop of yoghurt.

We often use these *bhajia* to make *Dahi Vada*. Prepare a bowl of whipped plain yoghurt salted to your liking. Drop the *bhajia* into a bowl of cold water and then scoop them out, squish them between the palms of your hand and place them on the yoghurt. Spoon over some more yoghurt so the squished *bhajia* are completely smothered. Sprinkle with some chilli powder and ground cumin, a handful of pomegranate seeds and a drizzle of *Amli ni* Chutney (page 151).

In Wembley there is a *bhajia* place called Maru's Bhajia House. Their signature dish is potato fritters served with a wonderful tomato chutney. It used to be a treat to go there after shopping for vegetables but as I don't live so close to Wembley any more I make my own version at home. They are really quick to make and the trick is to use the starch and moisture from the potatoes to make the crispy coating rather than making a batter with water. The potato slices will only be partially coated so don't worry if it doesn't look like enough flour!

Serves 6–8

3 medium potatoes
juice of half a lemon
1 tsp salt
½ tsp turmeric
1 tbsp crushed green chillies
3–4 tbsp finely chopped fresh
    coriander
60g gram flour
30g rice flour

vegetable oil for frying

Peel the potatoes and then finely slice them using a mandolin – they should be just a few millimetres thick. Place them into a bowl and toss them with the lemon juice. Sprinkle over the salt, turmeric, green chillies and fresh coriander and mix through. Finally sprinkle over the gram flour and rice flour and give it one last mix. The flour should barely coat the potatoes.

In a deep fat fryer or deep-sided pan, heat 8–10cm vegetable oil to 180°C. Drop the potato slices in one by one and fry a few at a time for three to four minutes until they are golden brown. It's ok if they stick together a little. Drain on kitchen paper and serve hot.

Serving Suggestions

Some people – like me – are dippers. I like these with the Tomato Salsa-style Chutney on page 151. Others like to layer the *bhajia* on a plate, spoon over some Tomato Salsa-style Chutney and *Amli ni* Chutney and then sprinkle on some more fresh coriander.

Bateta Vada are a classic wedding banquet staple. At weddings they almost always have raisins in them, which I really don't like, and so this is my simpler version. They are super easy to make and one of the few times I use garam masala.

Serves 4–6

For the mash
500g potatoes, peeled, boiled and cooled
1 tbsp finely chopped green chillies
1 tbsp grated ginger
1½ tsp garam masala
2 tbsp toasted sesame seeds
juice of half a lemon
1 tsp granulated sugar
1 tsp salt
3 tbsp finely chopped fresh coriander

For the batter
150g gram flour
1 tsp salt
½ tsp bicarbonate of soda

vegetable oil for frying

Mash the potatoes and then add the green chillies, ginger, garam masala, sesame seeds, lemon juice, sugar, salt and coriander and mix together well. Roll the mixture into around 15 balls. I make them just a little larger than a golf ball in size. If you have time, pop them in the fridge to firm up for about 30 minutes.

When you are ready to fry, mix together all the batter ingredients in a large bowl with around 100–125ml water. You want a thick batter which will evenly coat the mashed potato balls. In a deep-sided pan or wok, heat 8–10cm vegetable oil to 180°C. This is the only time I use a pan or wok for frying because in an electric fryer I find the *vada* stick to the wire basket and are hard to get off.

Drop your chilled potato balls into the batter. Scoop one out with your fingers – it should be nicely coated all over – and drop it gently into the hot oil. Repeat with a few more and then leave them to fry for about five minutes until they are starting to brown. Drain on kitchen paper.

Serving Suggestion

I like these with Green Chilli and Coriander Chutney (page 151), Lata Kaki's Red Pepper Chutney (page 150) or just plain yoghurt.

Variation

Potato Fritter Burger (*Vada Pav*)
If you have leftovers or fancy eating something a bit more substantial then make *Vada Pav*. Halve a small white bread bun, and spread one side with green chilli chutney, the other with red tomato chutney or red pepper chutney. Pop one *bateta vada* in between and *voilà*. You have a version of the classic *vada pav* from Bombay.

Bhajia

GUJARATI MASHED POTATO BURGER

Dabeli

There are stalls everywhere in Gujarat selling this snack. When I visited Rajkot, I never understood why my cousins waited in the ones with the longest queue. I would be salivating looking at people walking around with *dabelis* from other traders but they insisted on waiting at a specific one. Each trader has their own unique blend of spices that goes into the mashed potato mixture, and they knew which was worth waiting for.

Serves 1

10g unsalted butter or ghee
handful of leftover *Bateta Vada* mash* (page 54)
1–2 tsp *Lasan ni* Chutney plus more for the bun (page 142)
1 white bread bun
Amli ni Chutney or Green Chilli, Coriander and Coconut Chutney (page 151)
1 small onion, finely chopped
small handful of masala or plain roasted peanuts
small handful of pomegranate seeds
small handful of *sev*

* The quantity depends on the size of your bun. Once you cut the bun in half, the mashed potato patty needs to be the same diameter and about two to three centimetres thick.

Melt the butter or ghee in a frying pan. Add the leftover *bateta vada* mash and one to two teaspoons of *Lasan ni* Chutney depending on your taste. Gently mix and fry this off for three minutes. Keep stirring the mash the whole time as you want it to brown slightly rather than burn. Remove the mixture from the pan and shape into a patty.

Cut the bread bun evenly in half and spread one side with more *Lasan ni* Chutney and the other with either *Amli* or Green Chilli, Coriander and Coconut Chutney. Place your patty on one half and top with chopped onions, masala peanuts, pomegranate seeds and *sev*. Sandwich with the other half of the bun, and then place the whole thing back in the frying pan over a medium heat, gently pushing down to char the bread. Flip and repeat. Serve with a cold drink to take the edge off the heat of the chutneys.

FARSAN

Gujaratis are renowned for their *farsan*, which basically means 'salty snacks'. My Masis and Kakis all have their specialities and will bring them round when they pop over. I love the banter in the kitchen about whose is the best and which adaptations they have made with western-style tastes and ingredients.

At my wedding I insisted on homemade *farsan* for my guests and during the week before everyone — even the men — set about making enough for 1000 people. We had a production line going with Mum in charge of course. It was so joyful, with memories and stories of Tanzania being shared, and knuckles being rapped for those of us stealing bites.

SPICED, STIR-FRIED COLOCASIA ROLLS

Patra is one of my all-time favourite Gujarati dishes. My Baa used to make them for breakfast when I was little using fresh colocasia leaves that visiting relatives would bring over from Tanzania or India. I was too little to really appreciate her or her *patra*, which makes me so incredibly sad. However, I wasn't so little that I don't remember the wonderful smells in the kitchen and the taste of this lovingly prepared dish – though as a child I would ladle over copious amounts of plain yoghurt to stop the stinging of chilli on my tongue.

Serves 2–4

2 large colocasia leaves
150g gram flour
1½ tsp salt
1 tsp chilli powder
2 tsp finely grated ginger
2–4 tsp finely chopped green chillies
3 tbsp tamarind paste
2 tbsp grated jaggery
2 tbsp sunflower or rapeseed oil
4–5 curry leaves
1 tsp black mustard seeds
2 tsp sesame seeds
2 tbsp grated coconut
50g fresh coriander, finely chopped

Clean both sides of the colocasia leaves using a damp cloth, wiping carefully down all the spines to remove any traces of dust or dirt. Using a small knife, carefully cut off any thick parts on the spines, being careful not to rip the leaves, then set aside to dry.

Mix the gram flour, salt, chilli powder, ginger, green chillies, tamarind and jaggery together with a little water to give you a smooth, thick paste the consistency of peanut butter. Beat it with a wooden spoon to ensure all the lumps of flour have been removed. Taste and adjust the seasoning to suit your palate: if it is too sour, add a little more jaggery; if too sweet, add more tamarind.

Lay a leaf out flat on your worktop and spread evenly with half the paste then place the other leaf on top and spread with the remaining paste. Now roll it all up so you have a long cigar. Place this into a steamer and steam for ten minutes – if your steamer isn't wide enough, just cut it in half. Leave the steamed *patra* to cool completely; otherwise you will not be able to cut them cleanly as the paste will be too moist. When cooled, slice up into rounds about a centimetre thick. You can eat the *patra* simply steamed like this, but I like to stir fry them as follows.

Heat the oil in a wok on a medium heat. You can test if the oil is hot enough by adding a few mustard seeds: they should immediately fizzle and pop. Add the curry leaves, mustard seeds and sesame seeds in quick succession. Be careful as they may spit at you. Carefully add the sliced, steamed *patra* and stir-fry gently for about five minutes until some of them start to brown and crisp on the edges. Turn the heat off and stir in the coconut and freshly chopped coriander and serve with plain yoghurt on the side.

Tips

Nowadays I grow colocasia in the garden and at the allotment so I don't have to hunt it down. You should be able to find the leaves in bundles of ten in most Asian greengrocers. If not, try using chard leaves or thick fresh spinach leaves. You will need to use around four to six leaves as they are not as thick.

The fresh leaves come in rolls of ten so I often make a big batch and freeze the steamed *patra* whole or in slices.

Serving Suggestion

For parties these make great bite-sized canapés. Serve the steamed discs with a bowl of yoghurt mixed with chopped coriander and coconut for dipping.

STEAMED SAVOURY SEMOLINA CAKE

Dhokra

I am likely to upset many aunties with this statement, but I will boldly state that my mum makes the best *dhokra* in the world. On Sunday mornings we used to wake up to the smell of *dhokra,* pillowy soft sponges that I'd eat, piping hot, while I was still in my pyjamas. I'd get a smack round the head for being lazy and missing breakfast, and another smack for not waiting for the *dhokra* to cool, but I didn't care. It was worth it for this mid-morning snack my mum would be preparing for my dad. He didn't stand a chance. At university I'd take a break from nightly revision sessions to make these in our communal kitchen. The aromas would bring hungry friends and group hugs, making us all a little less homesick.

Serves 2 (or one greedy Urvashi)

250g coarse semolina
150g plain yoghurt
3 tsp finely chopped green chillies
1 tbsp sunflower or rapeseed oil
    plus more for greasing
1 tsp salt
1½ tsp Eno fruit salts
chilli powder for sprinkling

20cm round baking tin
wok or saucepan with a lid which
    will snugly fit your baking tin

Mix the semolina, yoghurt, green chillies, oil, salt and 250ml water together until well combined. Grease your baking tin and line the bottom with greaseproof paper.

Place some boiling water into a large wok and drop in a biscuit cutter or a small heatproof bowl. This is to lift the baking tin off the water for steaming – you don't want it to touch the water. Cover and bring the water back to the boil. When it's boiling, add the Eno to your batter, pour over two teaspoons of water and gently fold the bubbles into the batter. This will make your *dhokra* super light and fluffy so try not to over-mix.

Gently scrape the mixture into your lined and greased baking tin and place the tin into the steamy wok. Cover and steam for 20–30 minutes until the mixture is just starting to come away from the sides of the tin. Remove from the wok and leave to cool before turning out, slicing into squares and sprinkling with chilli powder.

Tips

Eno fruit salts is an unusual ingredient but worth seeking out. Mum always says *dhokra* is a great way of clearing out a poorly tummy and I guess that's because of the Eno.

If you are doubling or tripling the recipe, make each batch one at a time. This will help you retain the fluffiness. The key is to add the Eno just before steaming so you get that wonderful fluffy texture.

Serving Suggestions

Traditionally these are eaten as they are or simply dipped in oil with chilli powder and salt. I like to eat them with coconut chutney or garlic and chilli oil.

You can also pour over a simple temper of seeds. Heat two tablespoons of sunflower or rapeseed oil in a small frying pan, then add a teaspoon of mustard seeds and two teaspoons of sesame seeds and a few curry leaves. Let them fizzle and pop for 30 seconds before pouring them over the steamed *dhokra*.

If you have leftovers — maybe make an extra batch so that you do! — you can also stir-fry them in the same way as the *patra* on page 60.

Additionally, you can deep fry the steamed *dhokra* and serve with a dollop of yoghurt.

They make great canapés. I serve them as single squares with a spoon of chutney on top and a sprinkling of toasted sesame seeds.

CHICKPEA, ONION AND POTATO SALAD WITH TAMARIND CHUTNEY

Bhel

This is a popular street snack all over India. Where my father lived in Rajkot there are perhaps ten traders within 30 minutes' walking distance. It's a great Biting to have buffet-style so people can make up their own preference of ingredients.

Serves 2–4

400g tin chickpeas, drained
400g tin boiled new potatoes, diced
1 large onion, finely diced
100g tomato, finely chopped
100g sprouted mung beans (optional)
100g dry roasted peanuts
4–5 tbsp tamarind paste
1 tsp chilli powder
1½ tsp salt

To garnish

sev or Bombay Mix
Green Chilli and Coriander Chutney
   (page 151)
Lata Kaki's Red Pepper Chutney
   (page 150)
pomegranate seeds
fresh coriander

This is so simple – just toss all of the ingredients together so that everything is nicely combined in the tamarind. Then top with however much of the garnish ingredients you fancy. I'd start with a tablespoon of the chutneys and a large handful of sev or Bombay Mix. I also add in avocado, sweetcorn, grilled courgettes, sweet potato or whatever else is in our fridge.

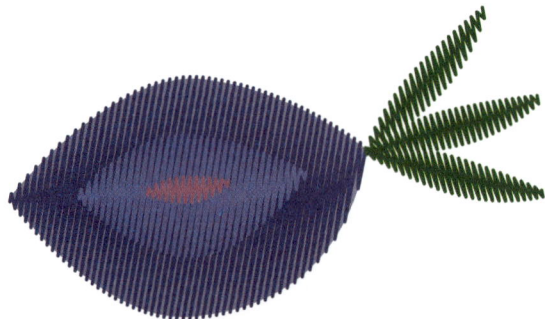

When I lived away at university in France, I'd fly through Marseille Airport on my way home and back. Because I was quite a regular, the airport security team got to know me. Empty bag on the way out. Full bag on the way back in. One time they made me open my bag. I had nothing to hide – it was full of spices and snacks from home, including these *chorafali* (I enjoyed them with red wine when I was studying late). The security guard had a taste, smacked his lips and there went my stash. On future trips I always remembered to bring him a batch. This recipe makes loads! Enough to keep you going through exam season. You can store them in a glass jar or an airtight container.

Makes enough to fill a 2.5l jar

450g gram flour
900g plain flour
1 tsp ajowan seeds
3 tsp sesame seeds
5 tsp salt
1 tsp turmeric powder
1 tsp chilli powder
1 tbsp grated ginger
2 tbsp finely chopped green chillies
150ml sunflower or rapeseed oil
   plus more for kneading

For the topping

3 tbsp caster sugar
3 tsp chilli powder
3 tsp salt

vegetable or sunflower oil for frying

Mix the flours in a large bowl and then stir in the ajowan seeds, sesame seeds, salt, turmeric, chilli powder, ginger and green chillies. Make a well in the centre. Pour in the oil, then mix it in 'til you start to get breadcrumbs. Now slowly add about 150ml warm water and mix to form a stiff dough. It should be the consistency of pastry or pasta dough as you will be rolling it out very thinly.

Oil the worktop and then knead the dough lightly. Take a large ball of the dough – about the size of a tennis ball – and roll it out so it's wafer thin. It doesn't have to be in a perfect circle because you are going to cut it up. Once the dough is rolled as thinly as you can – about 2mm thick – cut it into long strips about 1.5cm wide using a pizza cutter. Now cut each long strip into 4–6cm lengths. Place them on a flat surface while you roll out the rest of the dough in the same way.

Heat 6–8cm vegetable oil to 180°C in a deep-sided pan or wok. While the oil is heating, line a baking tray with some kitchen paper. Mix the sugar, chilli powder and salt for the topping in a bowl and set it close by to the baking tray.

When the oil is at temperature, fry off handfuls of the dough strips until they are light to golden brown and then drain them on the kitchen paper. Quickly sprinkle some of the topping over the *chorafali* and gently toss so they're evenly covered. Repeat until all the strips are fried.

Another Biting Biting staple for weddings and family functions, *kachori* come in spheres or disc shapes depending on who is making them. Two types are made in my family. One is stuffed with a sweet-and-sour *dhal* filling and the other with peas. This recipe is for the latter because I always have peas in the freezer. It looks like a lot of steps but once you get the hang of making the balls you'll whip these up in no time!

Serves 4–6

For the dough
250g plain flour
2 tsp sunflower oil or ghee plus
    more for kneading
1 tsp salt
1 tsp lemon juice

For the filling
250g frozen peas
2 tsp finely grated ginger
3 tbsp lemon juice
2 tsp cumin seeds
2 tsp finely chopped green chillies
½ tsp salt
3 tbsp finely chopped fresh coriander

vegetable oil for frying

To make the dough, mix the flour, oil or ghee, salt and lemon juice together with a fork and then slowly add boiled water little by little 'til it all clumps together into a firm dough. Pop the dough out onto your worktop and, with lightly oiled hands, knead until it is soft and smooth. It should not be sticky. Cover with a damp tea towel and set aside.

To make the filling, put the peas, ginger, lemon juice, cumin, green chillies and salt into a frying pan and cook for about five minutes until the frozen peas are softened. You shouldn't need any oil as the peas will release a little water as they defrost. Scrape this mixture into a food processor with the chopped coriander and blitz into a coarse purée.

Roll the dough into a sausage shape and divide into 12–15 pieces. Shape each piece into a ball and then on a floured surface roll out into a circle about ten centimetres in diameter.

Lightly oil your hands and then scoop a heaped tablespoon of the pea mixture into one hand and squeeze it into a tightish ball. Place the ball on a circle of dough, then gather the edges of the dough up around the pea mixture and pinch them together to seal at the top, twisting off any spare dough. Fill the rest of the dough circles in the same way. You can keep them as balls or you can flatten then into a disc shape.

Fill your deep fat fryer to the maximum line (or use a large pan filled with 20cm of oil) and heat the oil to 180°C. Take a plate and line it with two sheets of kitchen paper. In batches, gently place the uncooked *kachori* into the hot oil and fry for eight to ten minutes, turning if you need to, until they are golden brown. Drain on kitchen paper. You can serve these hot or cooled.

Tips

If you prefer, you can just roll the dough out into a sheet and use a biscuit cutter to cut the circles.

You may find it hard to make a neat ball. It can be a bit fiddly but don't lose sleep over it. Lightly score the circle in half, put the pea mixture into one half, leaving space at the edges. Then fold the other half over the mixture and squish the edges down to seal. It'll look more like a pasty but will taste just as delicious!

I have kept the filling spicing very simple but you can add a teaspoon or two of garam masala for a deeper flavour, or perhaps two teaspoons of crushed garlic and some chopped spring onions.

Serving Suggestions

My aunties always serve these with *Amli ni* Chutney (page 151) but it's entirely up to you. I like them dipped in plain yoghurt.

If you have leftovers, *kachori* make a good base for *chaat*. Break each one into halves or thirds and lay them out onto a flat plate, then spoon over plain yoghurt and scatter with *sev*, pomegranate seeds, finely chopped fresh coriander, toasted peanuts and sesame seeds. Sprinkle with chilli powder, amchur and garam masala.

RICE FLOUR DUMPLINGS

When I was pregnant with my first daughter Amber, there was one food that I craved above everything else. *Kichee.* It's simply a rice flour dumpling flavoured with cumin and green chillies. I think it was the sticky, comforting consistency that gave me so much satisfaction. It wasn't something I could make for myself at the time because the smell of green chillies would send me into a long coughing fit and give me nausea. But Across-the-Road Auntie would watch for my car pulling into my mother's driveway and within 30 minutes she'd bring over a plate of steaming hot *kichee.*

Serves 2–4

- 2 tsp cumin seeds
- 2 tsp finely chopped green chillies
- 1½ tsp salt
- ½ tsp bicarbonate of soda
- 150g rice flour
- 2 tbsp sunflower or rapeseed oil
  plus more for kneading

Pour 450ml water into a large pan or wok and bring it to the boil. You need space for the flour to expand when added so make sure you allow for that with the size of pan you choose.

Add the cumin seeds and green chillies and simmer for about three minutes on a very low heat. Cover the pan to stop the water from evaporating and minimise the aromas of the green chilli which might make you cough. Add the salt and bicarbonate of soda and then, very quickly, pour in the rice flour. The bicarb will make the whole mixture fizzle so make sure the rice flour is already measured in a bowl ready to use.

Let the water absorb the rice flour for a minute, then, keeping on a low heat, beat the mixture vigorously with a wooden spoon until it starts to clump together and form a firm dough.

Tip the dough out onto a large plate and drizzle over the oil. Knead it for about three minutes until it becomes smooth – the dough will be hot so you can start by using a spatula to scoop and push it down and then switch to using lightly oiled hands.

With wet hands, divide the dough up into eight to ten balls – I aim for something just a bit larger than a golf ball as my steamer is quite small but you can make them bigger if you wish. Flatten each ball into a disc and push a slight indent in the middle with your thumb.

Bring your steamer to the boil and then place the discs inside, leaving a little space between them as they will expand ever so slightly. Put the lid on and steam for ten minutes.

Remove the *kichee* from the steamer and leave to cool slightly before eating dipped in lots of chilli oil. If you don't have chilli oil you can simply put the *kichee* onto a serving plate, drizzle over a few tablespoons of olive oil and add a sprinkling of chilli powder.

Tips

Many aunties don't bother flattening the *kichee* into discs. They just steam the dough and serve it piled onto a plate and everyone helps themselves to scoops. I do love that way of communal eating too.

I make a wild garlic version of this. Add about 50–80g puréed wild garlic leaves to the water with the green chillies and cumin. Similarly, you can make a spinach version using the same method. You get wonderful shades of green *kichee*.

Traditionally this is eaten with oil or chilli oil – just pour five tablespoons of olive or rapeseed oil into a bowl and add one or two teaspoons of chilli flakes or powder. Or if you have *Lasan ni* Chutney (page 142) already made you can add a teaspoon of that to the olive oil instead. It's simple but so lovely.

SHAAK

In Sanskrit *saka* means 'vegetable' but in Gujarati it is the word we use for 'curry'. Depending on which part of Gujarat you are from, you might say *shaak* or *saak*. My family all say *shaak* except my friend Kavita who says *saak*. *Shaak* can be dry or with sauce, and it can feature a stuffed vegetable, single vegetable or combinations of vegetables. It is often associated with certain rituals or functions – for example, at weddings you will often see potato *shaak*, mixed vegetable and dumpling *shaak* and some form of *lilotri* or green vegetable *shaak*.

Usually on weekdays we have one *shaak* with *rotli*. On a weekend or at family functions we may have a few more. When I first got married my husband always got three or four *shaak* at dinner as he was the *Jamai* (son-in-law) in favour. Nowadays he gets one unless my mum needs a job doing around the house or garden.

There are three categories of *shaak*:

> ***Raso Varu Shaak*** *Raso* means 'sauce' and you can make any *shaak* 'raso varu' by simply adding water, passata or coconut milk either during the cooking process or the following day.

> ***Bharelu Shaak*** Bharelu means 'stuffed'. Vegetables that work well for this are aubergines and potatoes, bullet chillies or okra.

> ***Lilotri Shaak*** This is *shaak* made from green vegetables. Again, you can use single vegetables – say, green bean *shaak* – or mix it up as you like: green bean and pea *shaak*; green bean, courgette and pea *shaak*; green bean and spinach *shaak*, etc.

I make *shaak* about twice a week. I try not to have leftovers, but truth be told *shaak* makes such good Biting Biting the following day that I usually make double portions for that reason.

My mother was never so intentional. My husband's observation when he first visited my home was, 'Why does your mum have all these little bowls of *shaak* and rice and chutneys left over? Why don't you guys just eat that tiny portion instead of keeping it for tomorrow?'

The answer is simple. It is so that you ALWAYS have Biting Biting! If someone comes round unexpectedly then that small bowl of leftover *shaak* could be transformed into *parotha* or *chaat* or sandwiches. Nothing goes to waste in a Gujarati household.

This is the simplest version of potato *shaak*, the recipe I was taught at the age of eight. I was expected to be able to make this confidently at that age along with *rotli* and rice. After the recipe I've shared some ideas of what I do with the leftovers for Biting Biting.

Serves 4–6

1 tbsp sunflower or rapeseed oil
1½ tsp mustard seeds
1½ tsp cumin seeds
5 curry leaves (optional)
750g potatoes, peeled and cut
  into 2cm chunks
1½ tsp salt
1½ tsp ground cumin
1½ tsp ground coriander
1 tsp turmeric
1 tsp chilli powder
50g fresh coriander, finely chopped

a wok or a pan with a lid

Heat the oil in the pan or wok on a medium heat. After a few minutes test to see how hot the oil is by popping in a few mustard and cumin seeds. If they fizzle and pop then the oil is ready.

Add the mustard and cumin seeds and curry leaves in very quick succession. Let them fizzle and pop for a few seconds and then quickly add the potatoes. Be careful as the oil may spit at you – you can use the lid of the pan as a shield. Add the salt, ground cumin, ground coriander, turmeric and chilli powder, then pour in 100ml water, mix and cover.

Leave to cook on a low to medium heat for about 20 to 30 minutes. The potatoes should be just tender, not mushy. You can give it a gentle mix after ten minutes to make sure the spices are evenly distributed. Once it's done, garnish with fresh coriander.

Serve with *rotli* on the side or rolled up in a *rotli* like a burrito. I also like it on a thick slice of buttery toast because that's faster than making *rotli*. Alternatively, you can serve it with couscous, quinoa or rice.

Tips

Mix the cumin and mustard seeds and the curry leaves in a small bowl so they are easily to hand to add to the hot oil.

Use a metal spoon or fork to mix the *shaak*. My mum always berates my husband for using a wooden spoon because all the spices stick to it.

Don't be tempted to stir it more than once because you will break up the potatoes. If it is sticking, then add a little more water and turn the heat down.

Variations

You can switch the potatoes out for any vegetable you would like to experiment with. These measures are the base measures I was taught, and you can adapt them as you like. If you want it hotter then add more chilli powder. If you want a spicier version, then add more ground cumin and coriander. If you want onions and garlic, add them in with the seeds at the beginning. Nuts are a lovely addition to *shaak*. I love using peanuts and cashews. There are no rules, but here are some of my favourite combinations.

Potato and Cashew Shaak Add 100g cashews with the mustard and cumin seeds.

Potato and Peanut Shaak Add 50g whole peanuts with the mustard and cumin seeds and then 50g coarsely chopped peanuts with the potatoes.

Potato and Spinach Shaak Add 100g chopped fresh spinach right at the end. It needs about five minutes max to cook. Or add six cubes of frozen spinach with the potatoes and they will defrost as the potatoes cook.

Potato and Aubergine Shaak Add one large, cubed aubergine with the potatoes.

Potato and Pea Shaak Add 300g frozen peas with the potatoes. Make a double batch for easy samosas the next day.

Potato and Green Bean Shaak Add 300g chopped green beans with the potatoes.

Chip Shaak Cut the potatoes into chips rather than cubes and use two more tablespoons of oil and 50ml less water. This variation is my husband's favourite. Experiment with coconut oil or mustard oil for a different flavour.

Raso Varu Bateta nu Shaak
POTATO SHAAK WITH SAUCE

Tomato Raso

Make this in exactly the same way as Potato *Shaak* but add 150g to 200g tomato passata or puréed tinned tomatoes instead of the water. Mush a few potatoes right at the end and stir. This will give you a dreamy sauce for dipping *parotha* into or to have with rice, couscous or quinoa. I also like it on its own topped with feta and toasted sunflower, pumpkin and sesame seeds.

Coconut Raso

Make as per the Potato *Shaak* but add a 400ml tin of coconut milk instead of the water. And then stir in 50g desiccated coconut five minutes before the end. This is lovely drizzled with Green Chilli, Coriander and Coconut Chutney (page 151) and topped with toasted cashew nuts and rocket or shredded spinach.

Tomato and Coconut Raso

As above but add 50g tomato purée or 100g passata with the coconut milk.

SHAAK SNACKS

Shaak on Toast

ANY *shaak* is fantastic on toast. Make sure you cut your own thick slices – about an inch thick is good – of sourdough or ciabatta, or use a slice of toasted panini. The toast must be buttered before the *shaak* goes on and if you are a ghee fan like me then a few spoons drizzled on top works a treat.

Shaak Sandwich

I used to eat this at university when I got homesick because I always had individual portions of Mum's potato *shaak* in the freezer. After a night out it really is the best snack with a cup of tea. The sandwich works best with crusty white bread. Not anything fancy like sourdough but the ordinary white loaves the corner shop always has handy.

Prepare two slices of bread by spreading Green Chilli and Coriander Chutney (see page 151) on one side of each slice. Put three or four tablespoons of *shaak* on one slice and smooth it out to the edges. Add a layer of *sev* or some shop-bought Bombay Mix, chipsticks or ready salted crisps. Top with the other slice of bread, chutney-side inwards, and slice into two.

Shaak Parotha

These should be eaten straight off of the frying pan so they are a wonderfully social Biting. You can have one person rolling the dough, one stuffing it and one cooking. Serve with plain yoghurt or any of the chutneys in 'Chutneys and Pickles' on page 140 for dipping. Or top with scrambled eggs, toasted seeds and chopped fresh coriander. See page 132 for the *Parotha* recipe.

Shaak Samosas

There are lots of samosa filling recipes but I find it much more economical to use leftover *shaak*. Potato and pea or plain pea work well. You need some shop-bought filo pastry. Take one sheet and cut it widthways into three strips. Take one strip and roll it up so you have a cone in your hand. Stuff the cone and press down the open edge to seal it.

Baste the whole thing with sunflower oil and bake in a 200°C (180°C fan) oven 'til golden brown.

Shaak Chaat

This can look like a proper showstopper. You can experiment with whatever you have lying around. Slices of confit garlic work super well as a decadent topping. I also like scattering over toasted nuts and seeds for the crunch. It can be served with slices of toast or toasted pitta breads if you don't have time to make *parothas*. You can use hot or cold *shaak*.

Spread a cup of leftover *shaak* onto a plate. Finely chop 50g tomatoes and 50g red onion and arrange them evenly over the top. Put half a cup of plain thick yoghurt or skyr into a bowl and mix in a tablespoon of water and half a teaspoon of salt. Drizzle this over your *shaak*. Sprinkle over some *sev*, or some plain tortilla chips or ready salted crisps, lightly crushed. Hula Hoops work well! Drizzle over some chutney of your choice. Scatter with a couple of spoonfuls of pomegranate seeds and toasted, coarsely chopped peanuts.

When folks come over for a cuppa and a chat and then end up staying for dinner, Tin *Shaak* is almost always on the menu. It is simply *shaak* made using tinned beans or a combination with tinned chopped tomatoes or coconut milk. The combinations are endless but here are some I make often for two people. For four people I would suggest doubling up on the beans and adding half a teaspoon more of the ground cumin and coriander.

Tomato + Chickpeas + Coconut
Tomato + Kidney Beans + Coconut
Chickpeas + Baked Beans + Coconut
Tomato + Flageolet Beans + Coconut
3 × Chickpea or 3 × Kidney Beans

You can also add in frozen veg:

Flageolet + Coconut + Frozen Chopped Spinach
Tomato + Coconut + Sweetcorn

Please do experiment and let me know your favourites!

Serves 2

2 tbsp sunflower or rapeseed oil
1½ tsp mustard seeds
1½ tsp cumin seeds
5 curry leaves (optional)
3 × 400g tins of your choice per above
2½ tsp ground cumin
2½ tsp ground coriander
1 heaped tsp turmeric
1 tsp chilli powder
1 tsp salt
50g fresh coriander, finely chopped
   for garnish

Heat the oil in a large wok for a few minutes and then add the mustard seeds, cumin seeds and curry leaves (if you're using them). Quickly add the contents of your three tins, draining any beans or pulses first. Then add the cumin, coriander, turmeric, chilli powder and salt, stir with a metal spoon or fork, then cover and leave to simmer on a low heat for about 15 minutes. Garnish with coriander before serving.

Tips

Adjust the seasoning before serving. Brands of tins are all a bit different and some come unsalted so may need a bit of extra salt. Start with one teaspoon and then adjust as you need to.

If you are using three tins of beans or pulses you will need to add about half a tin of water to prevent the *shaak* sticking.

Crumbling in the contents of a standard teabag gives a nice earthy flavour to chickpeas and kidney beans.

Serving Suggestions

You can serve these with plain rice or *parotha* or *rotli*.

I also like making a sharing platter: topping a kidney bean or chickpea version with chopped onions lightly tossed in lemon juice and *sev* and then serving with nacho chips and dollops of yoghurt.

OTTOLENGHI SIMPLE
PLENTY
COOK · EAT · REPEAT
NIGELLA LAWSON
INGREDIENTS
JAMIE OLIVER
GRAINS
RAVE

We love baked beans and this is a super-quick Biting when you don't have much inspiration to cook. We all have those days when we just want beans on toast so try this version next time. It is especially good on thickly sliced toast with a fried egg on top. Or perhaps scrambled eggs on the side. You can add boiled potatoes also. It is our go-to Biting when we get home from a holiday abroad or when my girls come home from a school trip. It's quick and filling and makes the house smell fabulous.

Serves 4

2 tbsp sunflower or rapeseed oil
1½ tsp mustard seeds
1½ tsp cumin seeds
5 curry leaves (optional)
a few sticks of cassia bark
    or cinnamon
2 × 415g tins baked beans
1½ tsp salt
2 tsp ground cumin
2 tsp ground coriander
1 tsp turmeric
2 tsp chilli powder
half a lemon
50g fresh coriander, finely chopped

Heat the oil in a pan for a few minutes on medium heat and then add the mustard seeds, cumin seeds, curry leaves (if you're using them) and cassia bark. Leave to fizzle and pop for a few seconds and then lower the heat.

Add the baked beans carefully – because of the liquid the oil may spit a little. Add the salt, cumin, ground coriander, turmeric and chilli powder and throw in half a lemon – put in the whole thing, don't just add the juice (this is a nice technique that lets the lemon cook along with the spices and then you can squeeze in the juice just before serving).

Cook on a very low heat for five to ten minutes to warm the beans through and allow the spices to infuse. If it sticks then you can add a little water. Take out the lemon and squeeze the juice into the beans, then stir in the chopped coriander and serve.

I never liked aubergines at school. They were always dense, oily and tasteless, whereas at home my mother would stuff them with crushed peanuts, cumin and tomatoes to make these *reveya* which I couldn't eat fast enough. When I was younger, she'd send us all shopping so she could get the housework done in peace and quiet. We didn't have a car so we'd take the bus. Dad would spend aaaaages choosing the best small aubergines and meanwhile I'd have to watch my sisters to make sure they didn't run off. I guess this is why these were such popular snacks with all our family. Every aubergine was tender and soft, never bitter. Each a perfectly cooked mouthful.

Serves 4–8

100g blanched peanuts
100g tomatoes, roughly chopped
30g jaggery, grated
1½ tsp salt
2 tbsp ground cumin
2 tbsp ground coriander
2 tsp ground turmeric
2 tsp chilli powder
2 tsp finely grated ginger
100ml plus 3 tbsp sunflower or
   rapeseed oil
100g fresh coriander, finely chopped
12 baby aubergines
2 tsp cumin seeds
6 cherry tomatoes, halved

Preheat the oven to 200°C (180°C fan). Put the peanuts, tomatoes, jaggery, salt, cumin, coriander, turmeric, chilli powder and ginger into a food processor and blitz together. The peanuts should be coarse in texture so use the pulse setting so you don't get too much of a purée.

Pour this mixture into a bowl and add 100ml of the oil. Reserve a spoonful of the finely chopped coriander and then add the rest to the peanut mixture and stir everything together so it's nicely combined. The mixture should be like a thick paste so you can really push it into the aubergines.

Prep the aubergines by slitting them into quarters from the base and leaving the stem intact. Gently open out an aubergine and stuff it with a few tablespoons of the peanut, tomato and spice mixture. Repeat with the remaining aubergines.

Lightly oil a roasting tin or ovenproof dish. It needs to be large enough to snugly fit all the aubergines. Place the stuffed aubergines into the tin. If you have any spare mixture you can spoon it onto the aubergines.

Pour 50ml water into the gaps between the aubergines, then drizzle over the remaining three tablespoons of oil and sprinkle over the cumin seeds. Push the tomato halves in between the aubergines. Bake for 30–40 minutes. The aubergines should be tender and squidgy, oozing with the spicy mixture.

Tips

If you don't have a food processor you can crush the peanuts in a food bag. Pop them in the bag. Squeeze the air out of the bag, seal it and then bash the nuts inside with a rolling pin. Then add these to the tomatoes and spices and follow the recipe as normal.

Reveya freeze really well so it's worth making a double batch. You can reheat them in a 180°C (160°C fan) oven and then top with fresh coriander and crushed peanuts.

You can also use new potatoes instead of or as well as aubergines for this recipe. Slit and stuff the potatoes in exactly the same way.

Serving Suggestions

Serve with rice, *rotli* or *parotha*. This is how we would have them at home.

Nowadays I also like *reveya* with couscous, quinoa or bulghur wheat drizzled over with Green Chilli, Coriander and Coconut Chutney (see page 151). They are a great topping for toast paired with a poached or fried egg.

Scoop them onto a baked potato, sprinkle over feta cheese and fresh coriander.

Pop them onto warm garlicky yoghurt and scoop with sourdough slices.

MIXED VEGETABLE CURRY WITH BUTTERY BREAD ROLLS

Juhu Beach in Bombay has wonderful street food. You could spend the day walking along the seafront stopping to eat different dishes, but it's at night that the area really comes alive. My husband and I stayed on Juhu Beach and were treated to the legendary *pau bhaji* by our tailor. We had been put off by the queues so she sent her sales assistant to queue for us – I felt so bad but it tasted so good. This is my friend Pradeep's recipe and is a great way of using up odds and ends of vegetables left in your fridge at the end of the week so feel free to play around with the ingredients. This works best with shop-bought, soft burger buns.

Serves 4–6

1 red onion, finely chopped
juice of half a lemon
200g sweet potato, chopped into 1cm cubes
200g cauliflower, chopped into 1cm cubes
100g carrots
50g mangetout
200g fine green beans
50g baby corn
2 tbsp sunflower or rapeseed oil
1½ tsp mustard seeds
1½ tsp cumin seeds
3 cloves
1 large white onion, finely chopped
2 tsp grated ginger
3 tsp crushed garlic, crushed
100g tomatoes, finely chopped
500g tomato passata
200g aubergine, chopped into 1cm cubes
2 tsp ground cumin
2 tsp ground coriander
¼ tsp cinnamon
½ tsp ground black pepper
1 tsp chilli powder
3 tsp salt
½ tsp granulated sugar
50g unsalted butter plus a little for the buns
6 soft white burger buns
2 lemons, each cut into 6 wedges

Toss the chopped red onion with the lemon juice and set aside. Parboil the sweet potato and cauliflower 'til just tender and drain. Blitz the carrots, mangetout, green beans and baby corn in a food processor until coarsely chopped, or chop them by hand to 1cm pieces.

Add the oil to a wok and then put over a medium heat. Add the mustard seeds, cumin seeds and cloves and leave for a few seconds to pop and fizzle. Add the finely chopped white onion and cook for a few minutes until translucent, then stir in the ginger, garlic, chopped tomatoes and passata followed by the aubergine, sweet potato, cauliflower and the blitzed vegetables. Finally add the ground cumin, ground coriander, cinnamon, black pepper, chilli powder, salt and sugar. Stir so everything is well mixed, cover and leave to simmer on a low heat for five minutes. Add the butter and simmer for another five minutes. Give it one final stir and a gentle mash – the veggies should have retained very little definition so it's all a bit of a spiced veggie mash.

Split the burger buns and lightly toast one side in a dry pan. Butter immediately so the butter melts. To serve, pour the *bhaji* (spiced veggie mixture) into a large bowl and place the toasted buns and the chopped red onion on a serving platter with the wedges of fresh lemon.

To eat, take a toasted, buttery burger bun, spoon over a couple of heaped tablespoons of the *bhaji* and then sprinkle with the chopped red onions. Finally, squeeze over some lemon.

Angela was the first Italian I ever met, in my third year of university. Her family were from just outside Rome and, in the summer holiday before our final year, we travelled across Italy zigzagging the country using night trains to avoid paying for accommodation. The final stop was her family home where I first ate pasta with tomato sauce. It was so alien to me back then that I found it plain and I am ashamed to admit I added chilli flakes to suit my palate better. This recipe came about because I was cooking *shaak* in the communal kitchen as she was making pasta. She gave me some cooked pasta and I added it to the soupy *shaak* I was making. It worked and was a hit for us both.

Serves 2

3 tbsp sunflower or rapeseed oil
1½ tsp mustard seeds
1½ tsp cumin seeds
5 curry leaves (optional)
400g tin of chopped tomatoes
1½ tsp salt
1½ tsp ground cumin
1½ tsp ground coriander
1 tsp turmeric
1 tsp chilli powder
2 cups of cooked pasta shapes
    (we like bow tie pasta or conchiglie)

Heat the oil in a pan for a few minutes, add the mustard seeds, cumin seeds and curry leaves if you're using them. Let them crackle and pop for a few seconds and then add the tinned tomatoes. Be careful as the oil may splatter so have the pan lid or a splatter guard handy. Add the salt, ground cumin, ground coriander, turmeric and chilli powder, cover and leave the spices to infuse for five minutes. Finally, stir in the cooked pasta.

VAGHARELI PASTA

Grilled corn rubbed over with butter or ghee, chilli powder and salt is a fantastic snack. We enjoy it often. But when you want something a bit more substantial this is the *shaak* to make. The cashews add such a wonderful nuttiness. My husband will eat this in one sitting if I let him.

Serves 4–6

100g cashew nuts
2 tbsp sunflower or rapeseed oil
2 tsp mustard seeds
4 tsp finely chopped green chillies
300g floury potatoes, cut into
    3cm cubes
400ml tin coconut milk
1 tsp turmeric
2 tsp cumin powder
1½ tsp salt
3 sweetcorn cobs, cut into 6cm pieces
3 tbsp finely chopped fresh coriander

Toast the cashew nuts in a dry wok over a medium heat until they start to brown and fill your kitchen with a wonderful nutty aroma. Set to one side.

Put the wok back on the heat, add the oil and heat for a few minutes, then add the mustard seeds and let them crackle and pop for a few seconds. Next, add the green chillies closely followed by the potatoes.

Turn the heat to low and stir in the coconut milk, turmeric, cumin and salt. Fill the empty coconut milk tin with water, scraping down the edges to get all of the coconut, and pour that in, stir and bring to a simmer.

Leave to cook for five minutes and then add the sweetcorn and toasted cashews, reserving a few to garnish. Cook for another five minutes with the lid on until the potatoes are soft, the sweetcorn just tender and the cashews a little softened.

Garnish with the fresh coriander and the reserved toasted cashews, roughly chopped. Serve as is or with crusty bread, on rice or on quinoa.

Gujarati folk love a good *jamvanu* – it loosely translates as a dinner party. We used to have many when I was a teen and Mum would always make these bullet chillies as a classic but special side dish. It was one of the dishes I had at my engagement ceremony. I think the only reason she made them was to play a bit of Russian roulette with Tone to see which one would blow his head off. A little warning lest he not look after me I guess!

Serves 2–4

12 small bullet chillies
80g gram flour
40g jaggery, finely shaved
½ tsp salt
3 tsp cumin seeds
1 tsp *garam masala* (optional)
juice of half a lemon
4 tbsp sunflower or rapeseed oil
    plus 3 tbsp for tempering
2 tsp mustard seeds
1 medium tomato, finely chopped
5–6 curry leaves (optional)

Wash and dry the chillies and then trim any long stalks to about a centimetre. Slit them lengthways on one side to make a cavity for the stuffing and then set aside.

To make the stuffing mix the gram flour, jaggery, salt, cumin seeds, *garam masala* (if using), lemon juice and 4 tablespoons of oil together in a bowl and rub together 'til you have coarse breadcrumbs. Generously stuff a few teaspoonfuls into each cavity. Don't worry if you have some stuffing left over as you can use that in a moment.

Once all your chillies are stuffed, place a small pan or wok on a medium heat with the three remaining tablespoons of oil. After two minutes, add the mustard seeds and let them fizzle and pop before adding the tomato and curry leaves. Sauté for a few seconds and then turn the heat down to low.

Add 150ml hot water and simmer gently for a few minutes. If you have any leftover stuffing, stir in a tablespoon or so and then put in the chillies one by one in a layer – they shouldn't be on top of each other.

Cover and leave to simmer gently for about eight to ten minutes. The chillies will be soft and the filling inside cooked with a little thick gravy for dipping bread into. If you're lucky one or two of them will have burned a bit and you can have a sneaky cook's treat before serving the rest to everyone else.

Serving Suggestions

Sprinkle over fresh, finely chopped coriander and serve with plain boiled rice and *rotli*.

These make an epic sandwich. You want a soft, white, buttered bap and a glass of water handy just zin case one of them is a hot one.

Place on top of lemony hummus, scatter over toasted sunflower seeds or peanuts and scoop up with pitta bread.

When you literally have a bare fridge and are not in the mood for a complex cook, this is your recipe. It is guaranteed to fill the kitchen with a wonderful aroma and bring warmth and comfort at the end of a long, tiring day. It's fast to make and you can eat it unceremoniously with your fingers on cold leftover rice, crusty day-old *parotha* or even on toast or in a sandwich. We like it with torn baguette too. You can omit the ghee but I find it adds a velvety, buttery sheen, making this dish one you'll want to lick off your plate. Green tomatoes or tomatillos work exceptionally well.

Serves 2–4

2 tbsp vegetable oil
2 tbsp ghee
2 tsp mustard seeds
2 tsp cumin seeds
2 large onions, thinly sliced
2 tsp chilli powder
½ tsp turmeric
2 tsp ground cumin
1 tsp amchur
1 tsp salt
2 cloves garlic, grated (optional)
4 large tomatoes, halved and cut
   into 2cm slices

Heat the vegetable oil and ghee in a wok or large saucepan until the ghee has completely melted and started sizzling. Add the mustard seeds and cumin seeds and allow them to fizzle and pop for a few seconds. Quickly add the sliced onions and sauté them briefly so they are well coated. Add the chilli powder, turmeric, ground cumin, amchur and salt and then toss well so everything is thoroughly combined. Add a shot glass of water and the garlic if you are using it, cover and cook for five minutes on a medium heat until the onions are just starting to soften.

Take a moment here to inhale the aromas and commend yourself for making this epic dish.

Carefully fold in the tomatoes, then cover and cook for a further two minutes so the tomatoes are soft but still retain their shape. Eat immediately!

Serving suggestion

If for some crazy reason you have leftovers you can spoon the cold *shaak* over buttery toast and top with a fried or poached egg. Or this makes a great topping on hummus scattered over with toasted sunflower seeds and scooped up with pitta bread.

Variation

Ganthiya nu Shaak When we first moved to England, we lived with my dad's elder brother-in-law. He's the closest person I had to a grandfather and he made me laugh. He was always interested in what I was doing at school and made sure I was reading different books to broaden my knowledge. I don't remember him cooking when we lived together but his beautiful granddaughter Palvi recently shared with me that he'd make *ganthiya nu shaak* when he was peckish and needed some Biting Biting.

To make it, follow the recipe above and then add a handful of *sev* or a few bits of broken *Patta Ganthiya* (page 38) after adding the tomatoes. Also add half a cup of water at that stage. It should be a more soupy consistency so the *sev* or *ganthiya* are almost like pasta shapes in the fiery sauce.

Kishore Mama is one of my favourite Uncles. He's just so funny. He has the best stories of Africa and a wonderful chuckle that reminds me of Baa. He ran Pappa's garages in Tanzania until the 1980s and is a gifted mechanic and a fabulous cook. This is his adaptation of a typical Tanzanian dish that our farmhands and garage staff would make. It's eaten with a steamed maize flour dough called *ugali*. You mush the *ugali* into a disc shape and use that to pick up the *bharazi*.

Serves 4–6

For the *bharazi*
3 tbsp sunflower or rapeseed oil
1 small white onion, chopped
2 tsp cumin seeds
100g tomatoes, chopped
2 × 400g tins kidneys beans
    or pigeon peas
400ml tin coconut milk
1 heaped tbsp finely grated ginger
1–2 garlic cloves, finely grated
    (optional)
2–3 green chillies, left whole but
    slit lengthways
1½ tsp salt

For the *ugali*
350g white maize meal
1 tsp bicarbonate of soda
1 tsp salt

First make the *bharazi*. Heat the oil in a wok over a low heat and add the onion. Stir and cook until the onion is translucent, then add the cumin seeds and tomatoes and sauté until the tomatoes are mushy. Drain the kidney beans and stir these in with the coconut milk, ginger, garlic (if you are using it), green chillies and salt. Leave to simmer gently while you make the *ugali*.

Heat 600ml water until it just starts to boil. Add the maize meal, bicarbonate of soda and salt and stir until it starts to thicken to a mashed potato consistency. Keep stirring to cook the maize for about five minutes, adding a little more water if it's too thick.

Prepare your steamer and line each steaming compartment with some greaseproof paper. Transfer dollops of the mixture onto the greaseproof paper and steam for 15 minutes to finish cooking. It will look like a fluffy cloud of soft dough.

To serve, pile the steamed *ugali* dough onto a platter so everyone can help themselves to handfuls for scooping up the *bharazi*. I like rolling the heaped teaspoonfuls into rough balls and plonking them into my soupy *bharazi* – it's a bit easier to eat. But traditionally our folks in East Africa make the steamed *ugali* into a little flattened disc and then use that to scoop up the *bharazi*.

BBQ GREEN BANANAS

This isn't technically a *shaak* but it works nicely with the *bharazi* and *ugali*. It's a very simple Biting which Kishore Mama used to make at the garage on a makeshift barbecue. It would be eaten with a few beers, a few naughty Swahili songs and lots of laughter.

Serves 2–4

3–4 green bananas
juice of a large lemon
runny honey (optional)
chilli powder
salt

Grill the bananas with their skins on – either on a barbecue or a very hot griddle pan. Let the skins blacken on one side for about five minutes and then flip over to blacken the other side.

Slit them open lengthways, drizzle over lemon juice and honey (if you're using it) and then sprinkle on the chilli powder and salt to your taste.

DHAL

Dhal is the centre of the Gujarati universe as far as I am concerned. I cannot go more than a week without having it — especially in winter. Every one of us will make *dhal* in a different way with a different mix of spices so I'm sharing a version which is fast and easy to use as a base to build from. My daughter Amber doesn't like cumin so I know she will omit that when she eventually starts cooking *dhal* for herself.

I have also used the regular split red lentils instead of the oily *toor dhal* my mum uses. *Toor dhal* is time-intensive to prepare because it needs a good sort through for stones, a washing ritual and then soaking and pressure-cooking. I have a full-time job, two children, a husband, an allotment, a gym, yoga and social media habit and a very small freezer. I don't have time for *toor dhal*! Yes, yes, I know that Mum also raised the three of us on several jobs full-time and still found time, but I prefer split red lentils so let's just leave it there.

The *vaghar* (tempering) uses the bare minimum of spices I think you need. Aunties could argue over this for days but if you are a beginner then start here. If you want to go for deeper layers of heat and flavour then also add a few cloves, a star anise, half a dried lime, a few dried red chillies and a couple of garlic cloves.

Garam masala or no garam masala? *Garam* means 'hot' and *masala* means 'mix'. If it's a super cold day in winter and I feel we all need a bit of 'inner' warmth then I'll add a teaspoon. In the summer our bodies are already hot so you don't need it in my view.

I have seen so many recipes which use all kinds of vegetables in *dhal*. Traditionally, no, we don't do this and Aunties still find adding vegetables absurd but if you want to throw in some sweet potatoes or spinach or parsnips then go for it. It's a great way to get more veggies in your diet but I prefer to add them on top — see under Serving Suggestions.

Serves 4–6

200g split red lentils

2 tbsp coconut, sunflower
   or rapeseed oil

1½ tsp mustard seeds

1½ tsp cumin seeds

a few sticks of cassia bark

5–6 curry leaves

100g tomatoes, finely chopped
   or puréed

1 tsp turmeric

1½ tsp salt

1½ tsp chilli powder

2½ tsp ground cumin

2½ tsp ground coriander

2 tsp finely grated ginger

half a lemon

To garnish

toasted sesame, sunflower
   and pumpkin seeds

2–3 tbsp finely chopped fresh
   coriander

olive oil or ghee for drizzling

First, wash the red lentils in the same way as rice: swish them around in some warm water and then pour the water away. Do that a few times until the water starts to run clearer. Put the lentils in a bowl with some warm water and leave them to soak while you prepare the other ingredients. I find it's easier to have everything to hand when making *dhal* as there are a few things, so I line them up in order.

Heat the oil in a large saucepan over a medium heat. Make sure the pan you are using has a lid as you will need it later. After a few minutes add the mustard seeds, cumin seeds, cassia bark and curry leaves and let this all fizzle and pop for a few seconds before adding the tomatoes. Be careful as the water in the tomatoes may cause a little spitting, so put them in at arm's length using the lid as a shield. Reduce the heat to low and then stir in the turmeric, salt, chilli powder, ground cumin, ground coriander and grated ginger along with 500ml water. Bring to a gentle boil, pop the lid on and let this simmer away for about five minutes.

Meanwhile, drain your *dhal* into a sieve and give it one last rinse before adding it into the pan. Throw in the half lemon — you don't need to squeeze it, just drop it in. Finally add another 500ml water. Give it all a good stir, bring back to the boil, then turn the heat down to low and put the lid partly on, leaving a centimetre gap for steam to escape. I usually stick a wooden spoon into the pan first to keep the lid ajar.

Leave this to simmer away for 20–30 minutes. After this time your *dhal* will be ready to taste and season further as you wish, or serve as is.

I like to throw over toasted seeds and fresh coriander, and drizzle on some ghee or olive oil as a final garnish.

Serving Suggestions

Traditionally we eat *dhal* on the side of a main meal in a bowl like soup or with rice added in. But here are a few ways I like to eat it nowadays:

Sprinkled with roasted peanuts and eaten on its own as a soup.

Minestrone style with a few tablespoons of cooked star-shaped pasta or quinoa stirred through. For children you can use the alphabet-shaped pasta.

Topped with roasted vegetables, drizzled with olive oil and sprinkled with fresh coriander and seeds.

As a side soup for dipping cheese on toast into.

As a *chaat* with leftover samosas or *Kachori* (page 68): Warm up the *dhal* and ladle it onto a serving platter. Warm up the *kachori* and break them into bite-sized pieces, then place these over the top. Add some shredded spinach and chopped tomatoes. Drizzle over some yoghurt and scatter with pomegranate seeds, chopped fresh coriander and toasted peanuts and sesame seeds.

Thinned down a little with added *dhokri* – see *Dhal Dhokri* (page 106).

As *Dhal Parotha* (page 133).

As a leftover the next day: it will be thicker so warm it up slightly in the microwave, top with crumbled feta, toasted sunflower seeds, sesame seeds and sprouted mung beans, and eat it like hummus with pitta bread or chunks of sourdough.

Variations

To make a more tomatoey *dhal*, add a 400g tin of San Marzano chopped tomatoes instead of the fresh ones.

To make a coconutty *dhal*, use 400ml less water and add a 400ml tin of coconut milk and a tablespoon of desiccated coconut after you've added the spices.

Try using cooked whole mung beans or cooked adzuki beans instead of the red lentils, or even a combination of the three.

DHAL DHOKRI

This is a very popular Biting. *Dhokri* are pappardelle-like dumplings that you can cook in *dhal*. We used to have this on days Mum was running late from work because it's an easy standalone meal which takes next to no time to rustle up while the *dhal* is cooking and is very filling.

Serves 4

100g gram flour
100g chapatti flour
2 tbsp sunflower or rapeseed oil
   plus more for kneading
½ tsp turmeric
1 tsp salt
1 tsp ajowan seeds
1 batch *dhal* (page 103)

To make the *dhokri*, simply combine the gram and chapatti flours, oil, turmeric, salt and ajowan seeds with around 50–70ml just-boiled water in a bowl. Rub your hands with oil and then knead the dough for three minutes until it's smooth.

Divide into two balls and then roll each one out to 5mm thick on a lightly oiled worktop – it doesn't matter what shape you roll out. Cut the dough into strips about 6cm wide, and then cut it again in the opposite direction, so you have diamond shapes.

Once your *dhal* is cooked, blend it a little to make it smooth and thin it slightly with water if necessary to the consistency of double cream. Add the *dhokri* to the *dhal* and simmer gently for ten minutes to cook. Serve hot in a bowl, perhaps sprinkled with toasted nuts and seeds and freshly chopped coriander. It's such a filling dish that you don't really need anything else.

RICE

There are so many different ways to make rice and so many things you can do with it. In the main I use basmati rice. It's fragrant and has beautiful long grains. Brown basmati rice is now readily available too and it has a nuttier flavour. Traditionally, rice is an everyday dish — I don't remember not having rice as part of a meal when I lived with my parents. Nowadays I only eat it once a week but I almost always have some handy in the freezer as it's a fantastic base to rustle up some Biting Biting.

Mum and her sisters
cooking outside in
Dar es Salaam

Washing Rice We always wash rice before we cook it. The first time my English father-in-law saw me do this he looked on incredulously but I've never known any different. Washing removes the excess starch and as a result you get beautiful, soft, fluffy rice. Put the rice in the pan you will cook it in and then pour over lukewarm water. Gently, taking care not to crush the lovely long grains, swish the rice and water together to release the starch. Pour the water away and repeat a few times 'til the water starts to run clearer. This was one of my first chores as a child and I remember standing for what felt like hours repeating this process. It only actually takes a few minutes. Once it is washed a few times you can cook it or leave it to soak.

Soaking Rice Mum would wash and soak the rice in the morning, so it was faster to cook when she got home. You don't have to do this but even ten minutes is better than nothing. It will mean you have fluffier rice because more of the starch has gone through the soaking process.

Cooking Rice For four people I use 200g of rice. Wash it as above and soak it if you have time. When you are ready to cook, give it one final wash and rinse and then put it in a saucepan with a litre of water. Bring to the boil and then simmer for five minutes. Check a few grains of rice. They should be tender but still retain a little bite. If it's not quite there leave it to simmer for another few minutes. Take the pan to the sink, pour in cold water from the running tap and then drain the rice in a sieve. It should be fluffy.

Freezing Rice It's super easy to freeze rice. Simply leave it to cool and then put individual portions into re-usable plastic bags. To defrost, pop it in the microwave for a few minutes just before you are ready to eat it and it will come out lovely and fluffy.

Rice

MASALA FRIED RICE

Vagharela Bhaath

This is a super-fast way of jazzing up leftover rice. It takes rice from a side dish to a snack or light meal in itself. I remember this as an after-school Biting Mum would make before she went to work. We got home before she did and the cooled *vagharela bhaath* would be ready and waiting to eat with a dollop of yoghurt. I like it hot straight from the pan but it is also a good picnic Biting because it tastes great at room temperature too.

Serves 2–4

200g cooked rice
1½ tsp salt
1 tsp turmeric
2 tsp ground cumin
2 tsp ground coriander
3 tbsp sunflower or rapeseed oil
2 tsp mustard seeds
5 curry leaves
1–2 sticks cassia bark or cinnamon
2 tsp finely chopped green chillies
2 tsp finely grated garlic
juice of half a lemon
3 tbsp finely chopped fresh coriander

Mix the cooked rice with the salt, turmeric, ground cumin and coriander until everything is evenly combined.

Heat the oil in a non-stick wok for a few minutes on a medium heat. Drop in a mustard seed and if it starts to fizzle and pop the oil is hot enough. Add the mustard seeds, curry leaves and cassia bark or cinnamon sticks in quick succession. Give them a little swirl in the oil and then quickly add the prepared rice, green chillies and garlic.

Toss everything together and keep tossing for about three minutes while the spices cook out. You want to scoop the rice from underneath so you don't break it up too much, so use a flat spatula, push it under the rice and then flip it over and repeat.

Turn off the heat and add the lemon juice and fresh coriander. Cover and leave to steam in the residual heat for a couple of minutes to finish cooking. Serve immediately with plain yoghurt on the side.

Variations

Add 50–100g frozen sweetcorn in with the rice. I leave it there because I like the simplicity of the yellows but many aunties also add peas and carrots, shredded spinach, broccoli or kale. It is a good way to use up leftover steamed or roasted veg.

Add two handfuls of cashew nuts or peanuts in with the curry leaves.

Top with toasted seeds, fresh tomatoes and pink pickled onions.

My friend Henry loves rice and peas. *Mattar bhaath* always makes me think of him because I guess it is the Gujarati equivalent. I love it piping hot for brunch with a large dollop of yoghurt, and it's also a great base to have in the fridge for easy arancini when friends pop over.

Serves 4–6

250g basmati rice
3 tbsp sunflower oil, rapeseed oil
 or ghee
2 tsp cumin seeds
1 cinnamon stick or 3–4 pieces
 cassia bark
5–6 curry leaves
30g cashew nuts
2–3 whole green chillies
300g potatoes, peeled and
 cut into 2cm cubes
20g ginger, grated or finely sliced
1½ tsp salt
300g frozen peas

Wash the rice following the steps on page 111. Cover with warm water and set aside.

Heat the oil in a pan which has a firm-fitting lid. After a few minutes add a few cumin seeds. They should fizzle nicely. Add the rest of the cumin seeds, the cinnamon or cassia bark, curry leaves, cashew nuts and green chillies and then the cubed potatoes.

Now drain the rice and add it in. Toss everything together so the rice is nicely coated in the oil or ghee. Leave it to cook for a few minutes and then add the ginger, salt and 600ml water. Bring to the boil and then lower the heat, pop the lid on and leave to simmer for ten minutes.

Gently stir in the peas and then pop the lid back on and turn the heat off. Leave it alone for five minutes – the steam will cook the peas and fluff up the rice.

Toss everything through with a fork and serve piping hot with plain yoghurt.

Variations

I am a purist and like the simplicity of peas and potatoes, but Lata Kaki adds carrots and other vegetables for her grandchildren Ariyan and Amelia who love this variation.

To make arancini from cold *mattar bhaath*, you'll need some beaten egg in a bowl, some panko breadcrumbs and oil for frying. Roll a heaped tablespoon of the *mattar bhaath* into a compact ball, toss in the beaten egg and then coat evenly with panko breadcrumbs. Repeat with the rest of the *mattar bhaath*. In a deep saucepan, heat 7cm vegetable oil to 180°C and then carefully drop in the *mattar bhaath* balls. Fry them 'til they're golden brown and serve with Lata Kaki's Red Pepper Chutney (page 150).

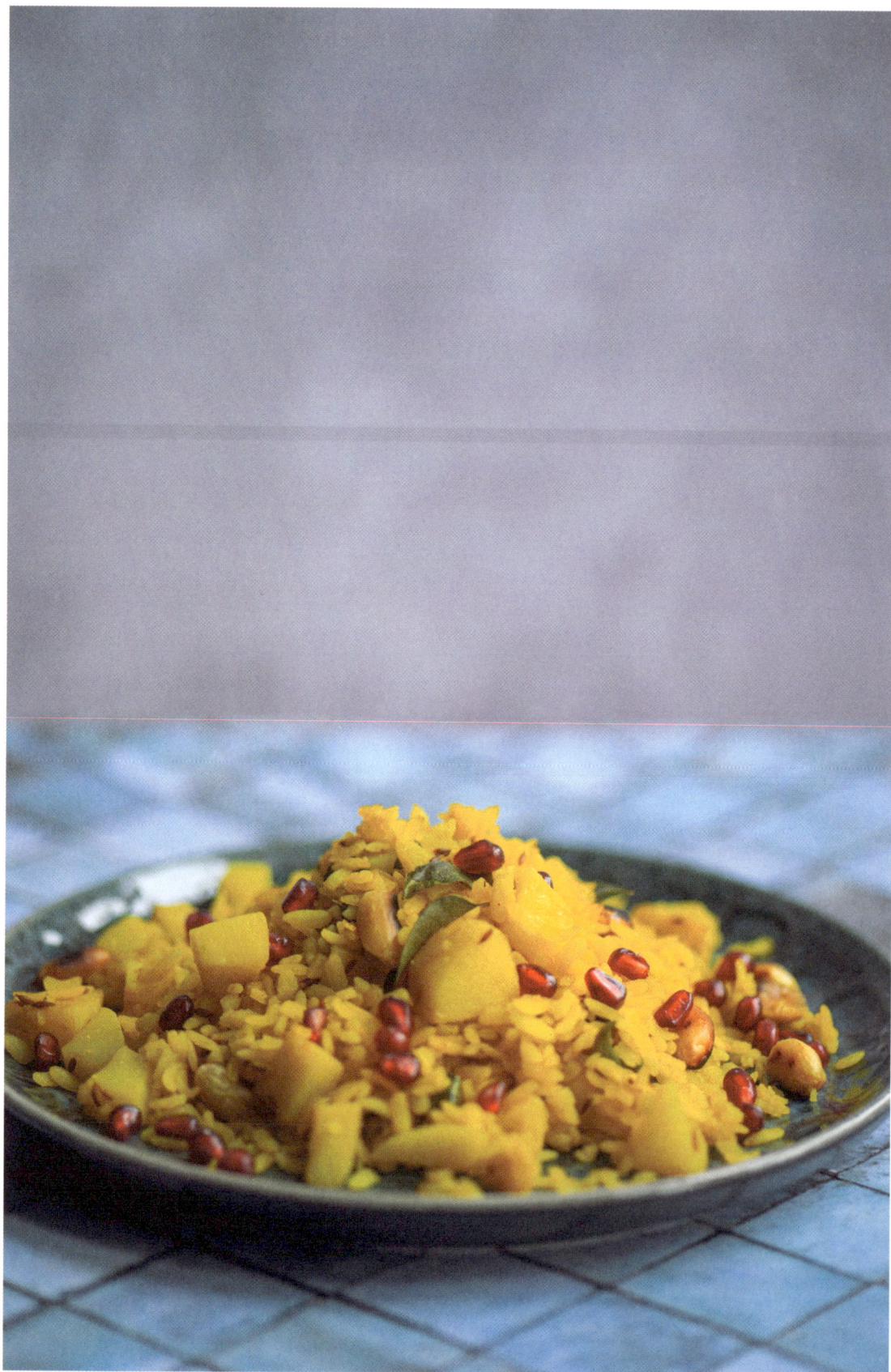

Pawa are dried, flattened flakes of parboiled rice which you can buy in most Asian grocers. They're very quick and easy to cook up and I've always got some in my store cupboard. Sometimes when I am really hungry but cannot be bothered to make anything fussy, I make this dish. On Sundays I make a double batch, to have immediately with fried or poached eggs and then to pack with some chopped tomatoes and onions to take to the allotment with a Thermos of tea. It's light, fresh and wonderfully fragrant and lures my girls from their beds into the kitchen. It's enough to keep them going 'til I get back from the plot.

Serves 4–6

50g sunflower seeds
300g medium *pawa*
50ml sunflower or rapeseed oil
2 tsp cumin seeds
10 curry leaves
200g potatoes, peeled and cut
    into 1cm cubes
1 tsp turmeric
1 tsp salt
2 tsp finely chopped green chillies
half a lemon
100g fresh coriander, finely chopped
20g toasted sunflower seeds
seeds of half a pomegranate
    (optional)

a wok with a lid

Toast the sunflower seeds in a dry frying pan 'til they are just starting to turn golden brown and set aside. Put the *pawa* into a large bowl, cover with warm water for two or three minutes and then drain through a sieve.

Heat the oil in a non-stick wok over a low to medium heat. After a few minutes add the cumin seeds. They should fizzle and pop but if they don't, give them a few minutes to do so. This is aroma number one. Add the curry leaves – aroma number two – and then the potatoes in quick succession. The lowish heat is important here because if your oil is too hot the potatoes will stick. Add the turmeric and the salt and mix 'til the potatoes are evenly coated.

Reduce the heat to low, pop the lid on and leave to cook for three or four minutes until the potatoes are just starting to soften. Add the green chillies and toss in the lemon half – this is aroma number three. Cover and cook for another few minutes until the potatoes are just tender.

Add the *pawa* with 50ml of water and squeeze in the juice of the lemon that was cooking with the potatoes. Toss everything together so that the *pawa* is evenly distributed amongst the potatoes. Cover and leave to cook for a few more minutes. Turn the heat off and let it steam with the lid on for a further five minutes. Pile into a serving bowl and scatter over the fresh coriander, toasted sunflower seeds and pomegranate seeds if using.

Variations

As with Masala Fried Rice (page 112) you can add in shredded spinach or kale and sliced up green beans or broccoli to make this a more substantial dish.

You could also use sesame seeds, pumpkin seeds or coarsely chopped roasted peanuts as a topping.

Many Ayurvedic doctors recommend seasonal detoxing and fasting – especially after periods of excess and/or rich food consumption. It helps the digestive system to rest, lets go of our attachments to food and also releases toxins that have accumulated, both emotionally and physically. *Kicheree* is the perfect food for this and has been used for generations in our family for nourishment during periods of fasting. Fasting in our Gujarati world is not about foregoing all food; instead we just simplify our diets or even – for some religious fasts – eat once a day. Mum says *kicheree* pulls toxins from the body and is healing for the digestive tract. It's eaten on its own or at the very most with steamed vegetables for those following a very strict fast. Some people add 'warming' or 'burning' spices such as ginger, clove and cinnamon. Interestingly, because it is so easy to digest, *kicheree* is one of the first foods given to little ones in my family. My mother used to mush it up with ghee and make little mountains for me to pick up. I have done the same with my girls when they were toddlers. It's also the go-to dish to keep our strength up when we are unwell. There is nothing like a bowl of steaming hot *kicheree* mashed with ghee and topped up with milk. It is also a perfect base for making lots of different Biting so we almost always have a batch in the fridge and freezer.

Serves 4–6

100g split green mung beans
100g basmati rice
1 tsp salt or more as to your taste (optional)
½ tsp ground turmeric (optional)

Wash and drain the mung beans and rice together several times under warm water to release the starch. If you have time, leave them to soak for about 15 minutes or longer.

Put the mung beans and rice into a pan and cover with twice as much water. Bring to a boil, add the salt and turmeric and then simmer until the rice and beans are soft – around 10 to 15 minutes depending on how old your mung beans are.

Serving Suggestions

My go-to is just plain *kicheree* with ghee and a touch of salt.

An easy Biting for when folks pop over is *vaghareli kicheree*. Use the same method as the *Vagharela Bhaath* on page 112 and toss through lots of chopped fresh coriander and toasted seeds. Serve with plain yoghurt.

Kicheree also makes fabulous *Muthiya* (page 118) and *Rasiya Muthiya* (page 121).

Variations

Instead of split mung beans use yellow split lentils. I usually add a teaspoon of cumin seeds to that version because I find it pairs well.

Add a clove of garlic, a teaspoon of grated ginger and some peas for a more substantial version.

OK, so this is not a recipe as such but rather an indulgence. When I was in the early stages of pregnancy with all the associated nausea and loss of appetite, one of the few things I could stomach was rice. Mum would give me freshly boiled rice laden with ghee and tossed through with sea salt. It really did restore my energy. I still have this as a quick Biting, especially when I am marathon training.

Serves 1

1 cup cooked rice
5 tbsp (or more as you wish)
   ghee, warmed
1 tsp salt

Mix it all together. For a sweet and salty version add shavings of jaggery.

Muthiya
RICE AND VEGETABLE DUMPLINGS

The smell of *muthiya* always makes my mouth water regardless of whether or not I am hungry. It's a really versatile recipe and no two aunties will make this the same way. You can use leftover rice or *kicheree* and pretty much any veg you have lying around. On my allotment I always have a bounty of beetroot and I hate to waste their vibrant leaves, so I'll often use them in *muthiya* and grate in some raw beetroot too. The *muthiya* come out a fantastic colour. Please do experiment and let me know how you get on!

Serves 4–6

200g gram flour
100g chapatti flour or wholewheat flour
500g grated/finely shredded vegetables (e.g. 200g cabbage, 100g carrots, 200g spinach)
300g *kicheree* or plain cooked rice
50g ginger, finely grated
2 cloves garlic, finely grated (optional)
2–3 tsp salt
2–3 tsp finely chopped green chillies
1 tsp turmeric
½ tsp baking powder
zest and juice of 1 lemon
50ml sunflower or rapeseed oil plus more for oiling

For the temper

4 tbsp oil
1 tbsp mustard seeds
handful of fresh curry leaves (optional)
1 tbsp sesame seeds
3 tbsp shredded or desiccated coconut
a handful of fresh coriander, finely chopped

To make the *muthiya*, combine gram flour, chapatti flour, vegetables, *kicheree* or rice, ginger, garlic, salt, green chillies, turmeric and baking powder in a bowl and mix well so all the spices are evenly distributed. Then add the lemon zest and juice and oil and slowly start squeezing handfuls of the mixture to bring it together into a dough. Take your time. The more you squeeze and mix the easier it will be because the veggies will release natural juices that help it all to combine. If you are short on time you can put it all in a food processor and pulse gently together.

Wash your hands, then lightly oil them and make golf ball-sized balls using up all the mixture. Make sure you press them together tightly; otherwise your *muthiya* with fall apart when steaming. Line your steamer with baking paper, then put in the muthiya and steam for 20 minutes.

You can steal a few while you wait for them to cool completely. I like them steamed like this and dipped in chilli oil. It's a cook's treat! Once cool, cut each *muthiya* in half and make the temper. Heat the oil in a wok for a few minutes and then add the mustard seeds. Once they start to fizzle and pop, throw in the curry leaves and sesame seeds in quick succession and then the *muthiya* halves and the coconut. Turn the heat down and gently sauté so the *muthiya* are nicely coated with the temper and then stir in the fresh coriander. I like burning some of the *muthiya* so you have a few crispy ones and soft ones.

Tip

I know two to three teaspoons of salt sounds like a lot, but the steaming process removes some of it so the end result won't taste over-seasoned.

Serving Suggestions

Chai and *muthiya* is a classic treat.

Make a *muthiya chaat* by spreading them over a platter, dolloping on plain yoghurt, layering on some chopped spinach and pomegranate seeds and then sprinkling over some toasted seeds or peanuts.

My favourite cousins are the Vadgama sisters – Saroj, Chandrika, Mina and Daksha. They are all exceptional cooks because their mum, Jaya Fai, was a strict teacher, even more strict than my mum who taught me to cook after I had done my O levels. My friends all went off on holiday but I wasn't allowed to go as I had to spend the summer learning a new dish every day. Mina is famous for her *rasiya muthiya*. Even our elderly aunties acknowledge her skills in making the tastiest version of this warming dish. I've adapted her recipe and used coconut milk because I love the creamy texture.

Serves 4–6

2 tbsp sunflower or rapeseed oil
1 tsp mustard seeds
1 tsp cumin seeds
5–6 curry leaves
400ml tin coconut milk
2 tbsp gram flour
30g ginger, finely grated
1 tsp salt
2–3 green chillies, cut into 1cm slices
2 tsp ground coriander
2 tsp ground cumin
15 steamed *Muthiya* (page 118)
juice of 1 lemon
5 tbsp finely chopped fresh coriander
1 tbsp chilli flakes
2 tbsp toasted sunflower seeds
1 tbsp toasted sesame seeds

To make the sauce you'll need a pan with a lid. It should be wide enough to fit all the *muthiya* on the base. Heat the oil in the pan on a medium heat for a few minutes, then add the mustard seeds and let them fizzle and pop. Then add the cumin seeds and the curry leaves followed by the coconut milk. Fill the empty coconut milk tin with water and then scrape the sides with a spatula so all the little bits of remaining coconut are not wasted. Pour this into the pan.

Add the gram flour, ginger, salt, green chillies, ground coriander and cumin and gently whisk with a balloon whisk until all the flour and spices are evenly combined and there are no lumps.

Turn the heat to a very low simmer and keep stirring. Because of the gram flour the mixture will thicken slightly. Once it does, gently drop in the steamed *muthiya* one by one. Spoon a little sauce over them and then pop the lid on. Simmer gently for five minutes and then squeeze over the lemon juice.

Serve hot sprinkled over with the fresh coriander, chilli flakes and seeds. The sauce is lovely mopped up with crusty white bread.

Ondhwo
RICE, SEMOLINA AND VEGETABLE CAKE

My friend Kavita always brings *ondhwo* when she comes over that she makes from a recipe that has been handed down from her sister Punita. Whenever I make this I think of her and one of her really bad jokes. It makes me smile. This is a very flexible recipe so use the vegetables here as a guide and throw in whatever you have handy, adjusting the water and cooking time by eye.

Serves 6–8

1 heaped tbsp sesame seeds
75g leftover rice or *Kicheree* (page 116)
200g coarse semolina
50g gram flour
75g carrot, finely grated
75g white cabbage, finely shredded
75g spring onions, chopped
20g ginger, grated
2 tsp salt
1–2 tsp chilli powder
150g plain yoghurt
4–5 tbsp finely chopped fresh coriander
juice of 1 lemon
1 heaped tsp Eno fruit salts

For the temper

20ml sunflower or rapeseed oil plus more for greasing the tin
1 tbsp mustard seeds
5 curry leaves

20cm cake tin

Preheat the oven to 220°C (200°C fan) and grease and line the cake tin with greaseproof paper or a paper cake liner. Scatter a heaped teaspoon of sesame seeds over the base and set aside.

In a large bowl, combine the rice or *kicheree*, semolina, gram flour, carrot, cabbage, spring onions, ginger, salt, chilli powder, yoghurt, fresh coriander and lemon juice. Add 200–250ml water and mix until you have a thick carrot cake-like batter.

For the temper, heat the oil in a small frying pan for a few minutes and then add the mustard seeds and curry leaves. Leave the seeds to pop for a few seconds and then pour the temper into the batter and gently fold it in.

Finally, fold the Eno into the batter very gently and then pour it into the prepared baking tin. Bake for 30–45 minutes until the sponge is golden brown, then leave to cool in the tin.

Slice up into squares or wedges and eat with piping hot tea.

BREADS

My late Gopal Uncle was a mechanic all his working life. He knew whatever there was to know about cars and could always be found tinkering on an old banger at the weekend. He was also a gifted artist. He painted the tins that I was gifted for my dowry: I keep chapatti flour in one and basmati rice in the other. Neither of these is ever empty. This is so that we can always have *rotli*, and when you have *rotli* you have plenty of options for Biting Biting.

WHOLEWHEAT FLATBREADS

No Gujarati meal is complete without some hot *rotli*. When my dad lived in Abu Dhabi, he took ages finding a local restaurant that made *rotli* the way we do. When we went to visit him, he introduced us to the owners so that if we got hungry during the day while he was working, we could pop in for a quick *rotli* snack to keep us going until dinner. The chef would make us *rotli* rolls using whatever curry was on the menu that day and wrap them in foil to take away so we could eat them on the beach. Ghee on top of a just-cooked *rotli* is not essential but it is *wonderful*. A leftover *rotli* is never left over for long because it's a perfect base for Biting Biting.

Makes 10

300g chapatti flour plus more
   for dipping
3 tbsp sunflower oil
melted ghee for basting

Put the flour in a large bowl and make a well in the centre. Pour in two tablespoons of the oil and lightly mix this in with your fingers so you have a few small breadcrumbs amongst the flour. Slowly add 250ml just-boiled water little by little, using a fork to mix it into the flour, forming clumps as you go. When you have a few large clumps, start using your hands to mush and squeeze them together. It will feel impossible at first but slowly it will start to come together into a firm dough. You may not use all the water. I find the process of making the dough quite therapeutic but if you are short on time you can pop the ingredients into a food processor and pulse. The first time I saw Dino Bhai's wife, Mina Bhabhi, do this I was in awe. I thought she was the coolest woman on Earth.

Pour the remaining tablespoon of oil over the dough and then knead it for five to ten minutes – depending on how much stress relief you need. It will become smooth and elastic as you knead. Cover it with a tea towel and leave it to rest for five minutes.

While the dough is resting prepare your workstation. You'll need a griddle to cook the *rotli* on, a small bowl of chapatti flour for dipping and a rolling pin.

Give the dough one more short knead and then divide it into ten equal pieces around 55g each. Roll each piece into a smooth ball and then dip it in flour. Flatten it with your hand into a disc shape and then roll it out to a circle about 7cm wide. Give it another dip in the flour on both sides and then roll it a bit more into a 12cm circle.

Put a griddle or frying pan on a medium heat and leave to heat for about five minutes. Place the *rotli* gently into the hot frying pan and leave for just a couple of minutes until you see some bubbles forming on the surface. This is what my cousin Daksha taught me to look for and I remember her wise words even now.

Flip it over to cook the other side for three to five minutes. You can use a piece of kitchen roll to press it down at the edges, making sure it cooks evenly all over. Flip it one more time and cook for a final three minutes, then take the *rotli* out of the pan and baste with ghee. Prepare the rest in the same way, turning the heat down a little after you have cooked five or so *rotli* so the pan doesn't get too hot.

Tips

Everyone has their own unique way of cooking *rotli*. I've taught you my way which involves a couple of flips but you can deviate from this. The main thing is that you check each side is evenly cooked through – five minutes on a low heat for each side should be enough. *Rotli* should be soft and not crunchy. It should fold easily without cracking apart.

Making *rotli* is an art. I've been doing it pretty much every day since I was eight years old, sometimes in batches of a hundred and sometimes just ten. So don't worry if you don't make perfect circles the first time.

Use a thin, tapered rolling pin called a *velun*. I've had mine for as long as I can remember – and I've been hit with Mum's a few times when I left the *rotli* to burn because I was daydreaming! The tapered shape makes it easier to roll a *rotli* evenly by applying pressure gently to the thick parts.

If it's easier, you can simply roll the dough to a few millimetres thick and then use a side plate to cut a circle.

I use my fingers to flip *rotli* but you can use a slotted turner. This is also useful for pressing down on areas that haven't quite cooked through or gently pushing down the top side when the *rotli* puffs up.

ROTLI BITING

Rotli with Ghee and Jaggery

This is the cook's and toddler's treat. Baste your hot *rotli* with ghee and then add shavings of jaggery or granulated sugar. Roll it up and devour quickly before anyone sees you. This secrecy is part of the joy!

Rotli Rolls

Leftover *rotli* and *shaak* make a great quick Biting. Lightly warm the *rotli* in a dry frying pan on both sides – not too much or it will crisp up. Dollop on some leftover *shaak*, roll up and eat with *chai*. For crunch add *sev*; for heat add fried green chillies or pickles or chutneys.

Fried Rotli

The ultimate Gujarati fry up. Heat some oil in a shallow frying pan. You want it hot – around 190°C – so when the *rotli* touches it, it immediately crisps up. Use tongs to push the soft bits of the *rotli* into the oil. Drain on kitchen paper and then sprinkle over sea salt. Eat with salted fried green chillies and pickles.

Vaghareli Rotli

My Amber loves *rotli* soup. It's what we make when it's cold outside and something warming and comforting is needed. This is why I always make more *rotli* than we need, so it can discreetly go and live in the freezer for such occasions. I say discreetly because if Dad ever found out that I freeze *rotli* I would be in trouble. His *rotli* must always be fresh – even for this soup!

Serves 2–4

200g plain yoghurt
50g gram flour
1½ tsp salt
1 tsp ground cumin
1 tsp ground coriander
½ tsp turmeric
½ tsp chilli powder
2 tbsp sunflower or rapeseed oil
1 tsp mustard seeds
5 curry leaves
4–5 stale/leftover rotli
2 tsp finely chopped green chillies
2–3 tablespoons finely chopped
   fresh coriander
2 tbsp toasted peanuts, roughly
   chopped
1 tbsp toasted sunflower seeds

In a large bowl, whisk together the yoghurt, gram flour, salt, ground cumin, ground coriander, turmeric and chilli powder with 600ml water. Heat the oil in a saucepan over a medium heat for a few minutes. Add the mustard seeds and cook until they start to crackle, then stir in the curry leaves and then the watery yoghurt, flour and spice mixture – it will fizzle and spit a little so do this slowly.

Turn the heat to low and bring to a simmer, stirring gently all the time. If you leave it at this stage it will split and possibly boil over, so the stirring is very important – this is Amber's job while I get on with other things in the kitchen.

Once it comes to a simmer, keep stirring and cook for five more minutes as it thickens – at this stage there's less risk it will boil over but keep the heat low to stop it splitting. Break the *rotli* into rough 6cm pieces and then add these in with the green chillies. Cook for five more minutes and then your soup is done. Serve sprinkled over with fresh coriander and toasted nuts and seeds.

SHAAK PAROTHA

There are so many recipes for *parotha* and so many varieties across India. Ours is very simple. These are usually a mid-morning Biting. On a weekend when a Masi or a Kaki or a Mami popped by after shopping, they'd disappear into the kitchen with my mum and after ten minutes the comforting smell of *parotha* would waft its way upstairs. No matter how much you wanted to concentrate on homework, it was impossible until you'd eaten at least one.

Use the *rotli* dough recipe on page 126 as a base to make stuffed *parotha*. You can use any leftover *shaak* but potato works very well.

Makes 6

1 batch *Rotli* dough (page 126)
½ batch leftover *shaak* (page 77)
melted ghee for basting

Simply roll the dough into an 8cm circle, place a spoonful of *shaak* in the middle and then fold the sides of the dough over to completely cover it. There are different ways to do this, but here is how I do it. Imagine 3 o'clock and 9 o'clock on the circle of dough. Pull these points up to meet over the filling and pinch them together. It looks like an Italian cannoli with the filling sticking out a little. Now bring 6 o'clock and 12 o'clock up to meet the pinch and pinch them together. You'll have four flaps at 1 o'clock, 4 o'clock, 7 o'clock and 11 o'clock. Bring these up and pinch them all at the top.

You should now have a sealed ball with about 1cm excess dough at the pinch point. Gently flatten it into a disc with the pinch point-side down, then dip it in some flour and gently roll it back out into a 15cm circle. Cook the *parotha* in a hot dry frying pan for about five minutes each side, until golden brown. Baste with ghee before serving – obviously!

As a typical student I didn't have much money so I always tried to stretch my meals where I could. I first learned this recipe from my Mauritian friend Marie-Noelle. I didn't know they had an equivalent of *parotha* in her country and the more we chatted the more I learned how similar the foods are. I sadly lost touch with her but this recipe always reminds me of our little talks in the tiny kitchen.

Makes 10

150g chapatti flour
200g leftover *dhal* (preferably with
    a thick consistency like hummus)
¼ tsp turmeric
½ tsp chilli powder
½ tsp ground cumin
½ tsp ground coriander
½ tsp salt
3 tbsp finely chopped fresh coriander

melted ghee or butter for basting
    (optional)

In a large bowl, mix the flour, *dhal*, turmeric, chilli powder, cumin, ground coriander, salt and fresh coriander together to make a stiff dough. If your *dhal* consistency is a bit looser than hummus then add a bit more flour. Give it a gentle knead and then take a golf ball-sized piece, roll it into a ball and then roll it out on a floured surface to about 15cm wide. Cook it on a hot dry frying pan for three to four minutes on each side until it is golden brown. Baste with ghee or butter.

I eat these with yoghurt, pickles and fried green chillies or use them as a wrap for coleslaw and salad.

Heral is one of my oldest friends. We first clocked each other on the 297 bus. I was going to school and he got on about three stops before Ealing Broadway. Of course, me being the good girl, I sat downstairs but he and his friends always went upstairs. He looked strangely familiar. I then saw him at a family event and had no idea that we were very distantly related. We spent a while trying to figure it out but then just started chatting about all sorts and have not really stopped since. He is like a brother to me and his mum was a cooking legend. Whenever I popped over, she was always smiling. Always. Even when she became terminally ill I only ever saw her smile. She was usually cooking something fabulous, but what I remember her most for is these *parothas*. They are epic!

Makes 6

500g chapatti flour plus more
    for dipping
2 tsp salt
2 tsp coarsely ground black pepper
70ml sunflower or rapeseed oil
melted ghee for basting (optional)

For the filling

400g mature Cheddar cheese, grated
½ tsp ground black pepper
3 tsp finely chopped green chillies

Put the flour, salt and black pepper in a bowl. Make a well and add the oil, mixing together so the oil is evenly dispersed. Slowly add 425ml just-boiled water, a little at a time, mixing with a fork to form a dough. You may not need all of it depending on your brand of flour. Knead for about five minutes and then set aside to rest.

For the filling, mix the cheese, black pepper and chopped green chillies together. Divide into six portions and make a compact ball with each. Put your (ideally non-stick) frying pan on a medium heat to warm up.

Divide the dough into six portions. Take one and make it into a smooth ball. Flatten to a disc, dip both sides in some flour and roll into a circle about 8cm wide. Put the cheese ball in the middle and then fold the sides of the dough over the ball (see the stuffed *rotli* technique on page 132). Press the dough down gently, dip it in flour and then roll it very gently out again to about 15cm wide.

Cook the *parotha* for five minutes on each side. Both sides should be nice and golden brown so flip again if they are still a bit pale. The dough may puff up, and if it does just flatten it back down using a slotted turner. Enjoy these hot from the pan, basted in ghee, with some plain yoghurt or pickles.

HERAL'S MUM'S CHEESE AND GREEN CHILLI PAROTHA

GRAM FLOUR PANCAKES

There are many, many variations of *poodla* across India and aunties will argue about measures and ingredients for days! The base they all have in common is gram flour and ajowan seeds. This is my mum's plain and simple version which you can use as a base to adapt and personalise. I've been eating these right off the griddle since I was a toddler – I remember I wasn't allowed to eat them until I was sitting nicely. Mum used to make these for my daughters when they were little too but *they* did not have to sit nicely. *They* were given a rolled up *poodla* in their hand and allowed to toddle around the kitchen. Memories of their little happy *poodla* dance – swaying their nappy-laden bottoms from side to side while singing 'ymmm mmmm mmmm' always make me smile.

Makes 10

150g gram flour
2 tbsp yoghurt
1½ tsp salt
1½ tsp ajowan seeds
2 tsp finely chopped green chillies
2 tsp finely grated ginger
2 tbsp finely chopped fresh coriander

sunflower or rapeseed oil for frying

In a large bowl, mix the gram flour, yoghurt, salt, ajowan seeds, green chillies, ginger and fresh coriander together and then slowly whisk in 100ml water to get a batter the consistency of thick double cream. You may not need all the water.

Brush a frying pan with a thin film of oil and put it on a high heat to get it hot. Turn the heat to low and pour a ladleful of batter into the pan, and then use the base of the ladle to gently smooth the mixture out into a round pancake. Leave it to cook for a few minutes. The batter will start to dry out a little and little bubbles will appear on the surface. At this stage, flip the *poodla* over and cook the other side for a few minutes. Eat straight away!

Serving Suggestions

You can make blini-sized *poodla* and have them as canapés topped with Carrot *Sambharo* (page 40), a pea-sized blob of yoghurt and a sprinkle of chilli powder.

They make a great wheat-free wrap for grilled halloumi, lettuce, cucumber strips and tomatoes laced with Green Chilli, Coriander and Coconut Chutney (see page 151).

Make a more substantial version by adding 50g finely chopped onion, diced tomato, shredded spinach, cabbage or kale. Add a tablespoon more yoghurt and a little water to adjust the consistency and about a quarter teaspoon more of the spices and salt.

This is a classic picnic Biting. We once went to Brighton with all the aunties. There must have been about ten cars following each other down the M3, none of them going above 50 miles an hour with the women at the wheel, so we must have driven the whole motorway insane. When we got to the seafront, we laid out all the blankets and then out came the *thepla* with various chutneys and *shaak* and Thermos flasks of *chai*. I remember us sticking out like a sore thumb amongst the other families who were eating fish and chips out of paper cones — longingly looking at them, wanting to be 'normal'. Nowadays we make a chip butty with *thepla* and chutneys and proudly devour it with a strong takeaway tea.

Methi na Thepla
FENUGREEK FLATBREADS

Makes 10

500g chapatti flour
1 tsp turmeric
25g pearl millet flour
25g gram flour
4 tsp finely chopped green chillies
¼ tsp bicarbonate of soda
1½ tsp salt
2 tbsp oil plus more for kneading
1 bunch fresh fenugreek leaves
    (around 200g), coarsely chopped

vegetable oil for frying and basting

Mix the chapatti flour, turmeric, pearl millet flour, gram flour, green chillies, bicarb and salt together and then mix in the oil. Add the chopped fresh fenugreek leaves and mix. Then slowly stir in 350ml just-boiled water, a little at a time, to form a stiff dough. You may not need it all. Lightly oil your hands and knead the dough gently for a few minutes so it becomes smooth rather than sticky. Divide it up into ten balls and roll each one out to about 15cm — these are usually a bit thicker than *rotli*.

Grease a frying pan with a little oil and place a flatbread down to cook for five minutes or until the bottom is golden brown. Baste the top with a little oil and then flip and cook for a few minutes more until that side is golden brown also.

As well as being a great picnic food with pickles and *shaak*, these are lovely hot off the frying pan with some cucumber *raitu* made by adding half a grated cucumber to 100g yoghurt.

Chevro is commonly known as 'Bombay Mix' but in truth we make it all over India. Every family makes it differently and as it is quite time-consuming we now usually buy it. I always have a jar on the shelf because it is an exceptionally good Biting. You can have it on its own or with lemon juice. It's great on top of leftover mashed potato, perhaps with some chopped tomatoes thrown on. It pairs *really* well with wine! And it is fantastic with cheese. As well as a stash of *chevro* I always have freshly baked bread in the kitchen as I am lucky enough to live opposite an artisan bakery. It's a good thing too because this sandwich features as a quick lunch at least once a week.

Serves 1

salted butter
2 slices crusty white bread
Green Chilli and Coriander Chutney
    or Green Chilli, Coriander and
    Coconut Chutney (page 151)
100g Cheddar cheese, grated
50g *chevro*

Butter both slices of bread and then slather on the chutney of your choice. Scoop the grated cheese and *chevro* on one slice and then sandwich with the other slice. Cut in half and eat right away. Don't forget to dip the crusts into more chutney.

CHUTNEYS AND PICKLES

An absolute must for Biting Biting! No snack is complete without a pickle or a dollop of chutney on the side. It takes things to another level. Mum usually has five different types of chutney in the fridge, or at least the ingredients to rustle one up quickly. Growing up, my least favourite job was preparing garlic for *Lasan ni* Chutney. I would come home from school to a sack of garlic and, much to my protests of too much homework, I was set to work peeling and pounding. We didn't have an electric mixer in those days so we pounded the garlic by hand before expertly adding the right measures of chilli powder and salt.

Another one we always have in the fridge is *Limbu Marchu nu Atthanu*. It's the Gujarati version of Middle Eastern preserved lemons. I love the way the lemons go soft and gooey. Similarly, we like fresh turmeric and a great way to eat it is preserved in lemon juice. I've learned other chutneys on my travels and am a particular fan of coconut ones. These I usually make as a fresh batch on the day, though they will keep for a few days in the fridge in a sterilised jar. They tend to dictate further snackage. So if I have made green chilli, coriander and coconut chutney then I'll almost always be making a cheese and *chevro* sandwich to go with it. The chutney comes first!

I'm not very good at Indian pickles but Across-the-Road Auntie did teach me a very simple base which I use for mangoes and apples.

GARLIC AND RED CHILLI CHUTNEY

Lasan ni Chutney

I grow a lot of garlic on my allotment. Mainly because I love this chutney so much and it works well with proper strong garlic as opposed to the mild supermarket bulbs. Try to seek out organic garlic from a farmers' market as you will get a much better flavour.

Makes 1 jar

3 large garlic bulbs
1 tbsp salt
3–6 tbsp chilli powder
3 tbsp vegetable, rapeseed
   or olive oil
1 tbsp lemon juice

Separate the garlic into cloves and peel them all. It's not a nice job so to make it easier, if you have time, leave the cloves in the sun or somewhere warm for a day as this helps shrink the outer skin a bit, making it easier to peel.

Put the garlic cloves into a food processor with the salt, chilli powder, oil and lemon juice and then blitz until you have a smooth paste. You want a purée with every piece of garlic completely mashed. Give it a taste – the salt should not be prominent but should just take the edge off the chilli and raw garlic. Start with less chilli powder and adjust to suit your taste. Transfer the chutney into a sterilised jar and leave it for a few days in the fridge or somewhere cool to mellow before eating.

Serving Suggestions

Dad has a spoonful on the side of dinner every day. He says it helps with digestion.

I like a spoonful in a bowl of yoghurt which I use as a dip for *parotha* or *rotli*. It's a great simple snack.

Thin the chutney down with olive oil or rapeseed oil and toss in some pasta. Sprinkle over toasted seeds, breadcrumbs and some parsley and you have an excellent quick meal.

It gives a nice twist to the Cumin-spiced Cheese on Toast on page 37. Spread it on the toast before you add the grated cheese.

Mush it into a jacket potato and top with cottage cheese.

On my wedding day I carried a little bundle of green chillies and a small lemon tied to my saree. My husband thought my mum had gone mad when she gave him a bundle to put in his pocket. Why? Well lemon and green chillies are a winning combination to ward off evil spirits. Perhaps this is why we always have this pickle in the house?

Makes 1 large jar

16 green chillies
8 small lemons
2 tbsp salt
1 tbsp granulated sugar
1 tsp turmeric
juice of 2 lemons

Slit the chillies vertically and remove the seeds. You want to keep them whole and intact but with the slit to allow the flavours to infuse. Cut the lemons into quarters and remove any seeds. Toss the salt, sugar and turmeric together in a bowl. Add the chopped lemons and chillies and toss together, rubbing the lemons with the salt and sugar mixture.

Leave to rest for 30 minutes, then add the lemon juice and mix again. Transfer to a large sterilised jar and leave somewhere cool for about a week. Every day give the jar a little shake to mix everything up.

After a week, the lemons should have started to soften and it is ready to eat. Once you have eaten all the lemons and chillies, just add a new batch into the same lemon juice. This way you don't get any waste.

Serving Suggestions

Obviously this is a hit with *parotha* or *rotli*.

It's also fantastic smushed onto sourdough toast and topped with cream cheese or cottage cheese.

Chop some up with yellow tomatoes and a drizzle of olive oil for a good bruschetta-style topping for crusty bread.

Blitz a spoonful into hummus and then layer some slices of the lemon on top of the hummus and top with chopped parsley and toasted sunflower seeds. It gives the hummus a lovely zing.

Chop it up with parsley and capers and mix with olive oil for an alternative salsa verde.

PRESERVED TURMERIC ROOT

It is becoming easier to find turmeric root nowadays and it is well worth seeking out. This is such a simple pickle but it's a really healthy thing to incorporate into your diet. Turmeric is known for its healing properties in Ayurvedic medicine and I always make sure I have this around in winter to ward off coughs and colds.

Makes 1 jar

15–20 turmeric roots
juice of 4 large lemons
1 tsp salt

Lay a few sheets of newspaper onto your work surface and oil your hands. The turmeric will stain both so these are protective measures! Peel the turmeric root and then slice them into a bowl – I usually go with 5mm thick circles but some people prefer matchsticks. Add the lemon juice and salt and toss well.

Transfer to a sterilised jar and make sure there is enough lemon juice to cover all the turmeric root slices. Leave to ferment for about ten days.

Katki Keri
SIMPLE CHOPPED MANGO PICKLE

Across-the-Road Auntie was always cooking. She's the only one I remember making these kinds of pickles. Nowadays most people buy them but I find shop-bought versions are too oily so sometimes I will make this recipe, which she gave me when I was pregnant. It is considered an honour to cook for a pregnant woman and she was always giving me food gifts.

Makes 1 large jar

500g green mango
1 tsp salt
1 tsp turmeric
3 tsp grated ginger
200g jaggery, grated
1½ tsp ground cumin
1 tsp chilli powder (more if you wish)

Peel the mango and slice the flesh from the stone. Cut the slices into thin strips and then small cubes. Mix the green mango, salt, turmeric and ginger together and set aside for 15 minutes. The salt will help to draw out excess water, which you can pour into a cocktail shaker along with 60ml vodka and enjoy as a strange but great Martini.

Mix in the jaggery and then transfer the mixture to a pan over a low heat and cook, stirring continuously, until the jaggery dissolves and melts. Be patient and keep it gentle. Add the cumin and chilli powder and cook for five more minutes. The pickle will bubble and thicken slightly. Leave to cool in the pan where it will continue to thicken as it cools before transferring to a sterilised jar.

Variations

I also like *chundho* which is a grated mango version made using the same method.

To make apple pickle, use the same quantity of firm, tart apples that will hold their shape – my windfall apples at the allotment work really nicely but I have no idea what variety they are so try Granny Smith or Bramley.

Chutneys and Pickles

This is a *fatafat* (super quick) pickle you can rustle up to serve with cheese or *shaak parotha*. It's also rather nice in a Brie sandwich and according to my Tone it is amazing with grilled chicken.

Serves 4

100g carrots
10 green chillies
2 tbsp lemon juice
½ tsp turmeric
½ tsp salt
2 tsp split mustard seeds
1 tbsp sunflower or rapeseed oil
2 tsp black mustard seeds

Wash and peel the carrots and cut them into 7cm sticks. Slice the green chillies lengthways and put both into a bowl with the lemon juice, turmeric, salt and split mustard seeds. Toss together well.

In a small frying pan, heat the oil for a few minutes and then add the black mustard seeds. Let them fizzle and pop and then pour them over the carrot mixture. Toss together well and serve.

Serving suggestions

Spoon a few tablespoons on to a *rotli*, grate over some Cheddar cheese, roll up and eat with *chai*.

Spoon generously over a bowl of hummus and scoop up with tortilla chips.

Use as a filling in homemade Maki Rolls – I know, I know, but it really works!

Toss a few spoonfuls into a bowl of rice and serve as a side dish to grilled tofu or paneer.

Gajjar ne Marchu nu Atthanu
CARROT AND GREEN CHILLI MUSTARD PICKLE

Coconut and Yoghurt Chutney

Serves 4

100g Greek yoghurt
100g desiccated coconut
3 tsp finely chopped green chillies
½ tsp salt
1 tbsp coconut oil
1½ tsp mustard seeds
5 curry leaves
2–3 small pieces of cassia bark

Mix the yoghurt, coconut, green chillies and salt together. Make a temper by heating the oil in a small frying pan for a few minutes, then in quick succession add the mustard seeds, curry leaves and cassia bark. Leave them to fizzle and pop for about 30 seconds to release the flavours and then pour them over the yoghurt mixture. Stir well to combine. This chutney is wonderful with the Black-eyed Bean *Bhajia* on page 52.

Lata Kaki's Red Pepper Chutney

Serves 4

2–3 long red chillies
1 red pepper
1 very small Scotch bonnet chilli
1 large garlic clove
1½ tsp salt
1½ tsp sugar

Blitz the chillies, red pepper, Scotch bonnet, garlic, salt and sugar together in a food processor to a purée. Thin with a little water to the consistency of your choice. Despite the Scotch bonnet this is not a very hot chutney. It's got a warming peppery flavour that pairs really nicely with *dhokra* and is delicious with cheese on toast. If you cannot find fresh Scotch bonnet chillies then add a few drops of Tabasco instead – which of course, like my boss Julio and my friend Pradeep, you must always carry about your person, always.

Tomato Salsa-style Chutney

Serves 4

2 large tomatoes, seeds removed
1 medium white onion, roughly
    chopped
1 tsp salt
1 tsp sugar
half bunch fresh coriander
    including stalks
tomato purée

Put the tomatoes, onion, salt, sugar, coriander and a squirt of tomato purée into a food processor and pulse until coarsely chopped.

Green Chilli and Coriander Chutney

Serves 4

100g fresh coriander
20g green chillies, stalks removed
juice of half a lemon
1 tsp salt
1 tsp sugar

In a food processor or blender, blitz the coriander, chillies, lemon juice, salt and sugar with 50ml water to a thick purée. You can water it down if you plan to use it for drizzling. If it's too watery, try adding in some bread or *sev* to thicken. Check the seasoning and then transfer to a sterilised jar. It will keep in the fridge for about a week.

Amli ni Chutney

Serves 4

100g tamarind pulp or concentrate
1 tsp salt
2 tsp granulated sugar
½–1 tsp chilli powder
½–1 tsp ground cumin

Mix the tamarind, salt, sugar, chilli and cumin with 50ml water together in a bowl. Taste and adjust the sweet/hot/sour ratio as you like it. This one is usually quite runny but if you prefer a thicker chutney then add less water. This one is perfect for Crispy Potato Fritters (page 53) or even for drizzling over *dhokra*.

Green Chilli, Coriander and Coconut Chutney

Serves 4

100g fresh coriander
20g green chillies, stalks removed
juice of half a lemon
1½ tsp salt
1½ tsp sugar
50g Greek yoghurt
50g desiccated coconut

In a food processor or blender, blitz the coriander, chillies, lemon juice, salt, sugar and yoghurt with 50ml water. Pour into a bowl and stir in the coconut. It will thicken slightly as the coconut absorbs the moisture, which is fine for pasting on sandwiches but do thin down with a little water if you need a drizzling consistency.

Tomato Chutney

Serves 4

400g tin San Marzano chopped
    tomatoes
1 tsp salt
1 tsp sugar
1½ tsp chilli powder
2 tbsp sunflower or rapeseed oil
5 curry leaves
1½ tsp mustard seeds

Mix the tomatoes, salt, sugar and chilli powder together in a serving bowl and set aside. Heat the oil in a small frying pan and then add the curry leaves and mustard seeds. Let them fizzle and pop and then pour them over the tomato mixture. Stir well.

SWEET BITING

Biting Biting doesn't have to be savoury. Gujaratis are famous for their sweet tooth. As children we are encouraged to take a bite of something sweet to quash the heat on our tongues rather than sip water. This could simply be a piece of jaggery or some fruit. I especially liked mangoes and pomegranates. When we were lucky it was a nice pudding.

I am a sucker for Sweet Bitings which are often handed out as *prasad* at temples. These are offerings made to the deities and then shared amongst the devotees. This was always my favourite part of going to the temple as a child. I remember my Dad or Govind Bapa carrying me up to ding the bell on entry and then I would patiently sit through all the hymns and sermons and prayers – *aarti* – with the promise of *penda* or *burfi* at the end.

Mithee Sev
MUM'S SWEET VERMICELLI

This is my mother's speciality — vermicelli sweetened with jaggery or sugar and spiced with nuts and cardamom. Sometimes when my cousins came to stay we'd have this in warmed milk as midnight Biting Biting. I remember piling all our duvets on the floor of the living room to make a communal bed and then we'd stay up late slurping this sweet *sev*.

Serves 2–6

25g ghee or unsalted butter
100g vermicelli noodles
3 tbsp brown sugar
½ tsp ground cardamom
1½ tsp vanilla extract
2 tbsp flaked almonds or chopped
   pistachios (or a combination
   of both)

Heat the ghee or butter in a thick bottomed frying pan on a low heat and when it's just melted break in the vermicelli noodles. Toss them well in the ghee and then keep stirring them gently until they are nicely browned.

Add 200ml water and the brown sugar, give it a stir so the sugar is evenly combined with the noodles, and simmer gently for about ten minutes until the water is all absorbed and the noodles are soft. Stir in the cardamom and vanilla and cook for another three to five minutes. If it sticks you can add a little more water so it doesn't burn. Serve hot, sprinkled with the nuts.

Variations

I sometimes add 100ml double cream at the same time as the cardamom and vanilla for a more indulgent version.

If you are making this for children, try using different noodle shapes. My girls used to like alphabet pasta and stars when they were toddlers.

Sweet Biting

CARDAMOM-SPICED YOGHURT

Fatafat Shrikhand

Shrikhand is perhaps my all-time favouritest ever dessert. I served it at my wedding and I think I probably ate more than anybody else. It's thick, sweetened yoghurt spiced with cardamom, and at weddings it will also have saffron added. Socks Auntie is the queen of *shrikhand*. She makes it the traditional way, which involves laying the yoghurt on muslin on top of a thick wad of newspapers. This is left for hours and hours so the water drains out, leaving a thick curd which she then scoops into a bowl and finishes off with a sugar syrup and the spices. I don't have the patience to wait hours so here is a faster version. I call it by her phrase *fatafat* for this reason. It means 'super-duper speedy'.

Serve 1–2

180g cream cheese or *labneh*
150g thick Greek yoghurt
¾ tsp ground cardamom
1 vanilla pod
60g icing sugar, sieved
2 tbsp toasted flaked almonds
or finely sliced pistachios
2 tbsp pomegranate seeds
(optional)

Put the cream cheese, yoghurt and cardamom into a bowl. Split the vanilla pod and scrape the seeds into the bowl, then add the icing sugar and mix well. Top with the nuts and pomegranates.

It is literally that – *fatafat*!

When we were little, every Friday Dad would bring us pockets of treats. It was almost always Smarties or fudge. I would save mine to last the week but my sisters would finish theirs there and then. This fudge reminds me of those happy Fridays. It is a super quick, sweet Biting that you can rustle up to have warm with tea or coffee. It's incredibly moreish. I could eat the whole batch by myself. It also makes great petit fours served with a small bowl of melted chocolate.

Makes 20–24 squares

100g ghee plus more for greasing
50g sesame seeds
150g jaggery
200g chapatti flour

20cm square baking tin

Grease your baking tin with ghee. Toast the sesame seeds in a dry pan and set aside. Cut the jaggery into thin flakes or shavings and set aside.

Melt half the ghee in a large frying pan over a low heat, then stir in the flour and toast it for about five minutes. Do this while continuously stirring because otherwise it will catch and burn. (If you think it's burning, whip the pan off the heat, stir and pop it back.)

Take the pan off the heat, add the toasted sesame seeds and then tip the mixture into a bowl.

Melt the remaining ghee in the pan over a very low heat and add the jaggery. Keep stirring while the jaggery melts and starts to bubble to make sure it doesn't burn. As soon as it starts to darken, add the flour and sesame mixture and combine well.

Cook for one more minute and then tip it into the greased tin, flatten out and cut into pieces with a sharp knife. Work as quickly as you can transferring it to the greased tin. It hardens as it cools and depending on the temperature in your kitchen this might be sooner than you think! Don't worry if this happens as you can pop the mixture in the microwave for a burst and it should soften up again. Leave to cool for about ten minutes before eating.

Ghor Papdi
JAGGERY FUDGE WITH SESAME

KARAMSI'S SEMOLINA PUDDING

One of the rituals Kishore Mama still observes is sending food up to the elders on the anniversary of their death. Pappa did this for my great grandfather Karamsi and now Mama carries on the tradition. The food is always this *seero* because that was his favourite. We leave it in the garden for the birds and animals to take to him.

Serves 6–10

150g ghee
200g coarse semolina
200g soft brown sugar
¾ tsp cardamom
150ml double cream
2–3 tbsp rose syrup (optional)
2–3 tbsp toasted flaked almonds and
 dried rose petals for garnish

Melt the ghee in a thick-bottomed pan over a low heat. When it's just melted add the semolina and keep stirring with a wooden spoon until it has started to brown. I usually stir a bit over the heat and then off the heat so it has no chance of burning. Once it has evenly browned, add 500ml hot water – careful here as it may spit, so go slowly.

Stir in the sugar and leave it to simmer gently for about five to ten minutes until it's nice and thick and all the sugar has dissolved (you may need to stir it from time to time to ensure it is). Finally stir in the cardamom and cream and cook for another three to five minutes. At this stage you can stir in the rose syrup (if you're using it).

Take the pan off the heat and let the *seero* cool a little before serving with the flaked almonds and dried rose petals over the top. It might clump up as you transfer it out of the pan, but you can simply use a fork to break up the lumps again.

Serving Suggestions

I sometimes omit the cream and serve the *seero* with vanilla custard or ice cream.

To serve as little petit fours, let the *seero* cool and roll it into balls. Place a flaked almond and dried rose petal on top and serve on a bed of fresh rose petals.

For dessert canapés, scoop the *seero* into ready-made mini pastry cases and pipe over freshly whipped cream or Italian meringue sprinkled lightly with ground cardamom.

MILLIONAIRE'S BURFI

My girls love *burfi*. Whenever we go to weddings or religious functions I seek out the *penda* and they seek out the *burfi*. They also love millionaire's shortbread so we came up with this recipe that covers both.

Makes 12–24

120ml ghee
240ml full fat milk
500g milk powder
100g icing sugar, sieved
ready–made drizzling caramel
   (salted if you prefer)
chocolate sprinkles or shavings

20cm square baking tin

Grease and line your tin with greaseproof paper. Put the ghee in a pan and when it has just melted add the milk. Gently whisk together so they are well combined. Add the milk powder, set a timer for five minutes and stir, stir, stir and mash, mash, mash! This process cooks out the milk powder. Don't worry if the ghee and milk solids separate; keep stirring and mashing for the full five minutes. Stir in the icing sugar until it's combined.

Transfer the mixture to a free-standing mixer with a paddle attachment and mix for three more minutes. It will soften up like creamed butter and sugar and you will be left with fluffy, soft *burfi* mixture to transfer to your prepared tin. Smooth and level the mixture in the tin using the back of a metal spoon or a palate knife and then leave to set for about 30 minutes.

Turn the *burfi* out of the tin onto a serving platter or chopping board. Cut it into 3cm squares. Layer over a few tablespoons of caramel and then sprinkle over the chocolate shavings/sprinkles. Alternatively, you can cut the *burfi* into slightly smaller squares and then serve with cocktail sticks, a bowl of caramel and a bowl of chocolate sprinkles so your guests can take a dip into each, taking as much or as little as they would like.

Every year on Boxing Day we have friends over to our house. One year I made these brownies and I gave the children a puzzle. I gave them the numbers 200, 200, 200, 3 and 50. If they could match the numbers with ingredients then they could eat the brownies. It took them a couple of hours but they got there in the end.

Makes 9 large slices

200g unsalted butter
200g dark chocolate
200g caster sugar
3 large eggs
50g chapatti flour
1 tbsp vanilla extract
250g fresh or frozen cranberries
   or raspberries
edible glitter (optional)

20cm square cake tin

Pop the oven on to 180°C (160°C fan) and grease your cake tin. Melt the butter and chocolate in a heatproof bowl. I do this in 30 second bursts in the microwave but you can also put the bowl over a pan of simmering water. Set aside to cool.

Whisk the caster sugar and the eggs for about five minutes until they thicken and foam. Pour in the cooled chocolate and butter mixture and gently fold it in. Add the flour and vanilla extract and fold again until all traces of flour have gone. Spoon the mixture into the prepared cake tin and then scatter over the berries. Bake for 40 minutes and then leave to cool in the tin. Sprinkle over edible glitter before cutting into squares and serving with vanilla ice cream.

When I lived in Aix-en-Provence I worked in a little café right on the Cours Mirabeau. They made the most delicious chocolate mousse. I thought it must be a labour of love until Chef showed me how quick it was to make. It's very rich so I serve this in Grandma Millie's posh coupe glasses.

Serves 6

300g dark chocolate
 (at least 80% cocoa)
300ml double cream
3 large egg whites
1 tbsp granulated sugar
ground cardamom for sprinkling
frozen raspberries (optional)

Melt the dark chocolate either in the microwave or in a bowl over a pan of simmering water and set aside. Whisk the cream until you have pillowy soft peaks. Whisk the egg whites to stiff peaks, then add the sugar and whisk again for a minute. Using a spatula, fold the melted chocolate into the cream a little at a time. Gently fold in a spoonful of the whisked egg whites, then fold in the rest, bit by bit. Be very gentle as you want to keep it light and fluffy and not knock out any of the air.

Spoon into coupe or Martini glasses and sprinkle over a pinch of cardamom. Sometimes I also crumble over some frozen raspberries just before serving.

CHOCOLATE AND CARDAMOM MOUSSE

I don't have too many memories of Tanzania but I do remember the soldiers and their guns. Brave smiles when we walked past them. Hushed conversations between the adults. My family's migration was later than the first political evictions in Uganda and perhaps less brutal based on the stories I've heard from my elders and friends. But it was brutal nonetheless. The climate for Indians suddenly became quite hostile with restrictions on trade and curfews imposed. Random house checks at the whim of the army were common and terrifying for us all. Memories of soldiers, therefore, have always been pushed to the back of my mind and until I was an adult I never gave much thought to the African folks we left behind. We worked hand in hand with farmers and labourers. Pappa supported many local villages with food and equipment drops. It's likely that the children were as disinterested as I was in the politics and madness which overtook the country and felt just as lost and confused. I know Pappa always took sweets for them when he visited the villages and I think of them whenever I make this recipe. *Penda* are usually flavoured with cardamom or saffron but I use vanilla which grows beautifully in East Africa.

Makes 12

60g unsalted butter
200ml condensed milk
100g milk powder
seeds of 2 vanilla pods

In a heavy-bottomed pan, melt the butter over a low heat. Add the condensed milk and milk powder and stir continuously until you get a thick paste – set the timer for ten minutes. You must keep the heat very low to avoid it sticking and burning. After ten minutes turn the heat off and scrape the mixture onto a plate to cool until it's comfortable to touch.

Flatten out the doughy mixture slightly. Scrape out the seeds from the vanilla pods and smooth them onto the top, then gently knead in so they are evenly distributed. Roll the mixture into 12 equal balls.

Roll each ball in the palm of your hand until it's smooth – it helps to lightly grease your hands with melted butter to prevent sticking.

Flatten the balls into fat discs and then roll them over the ridges of a fork or gnocchi maker to get a ridged pattern on the sides. Or you can simply imprint a nice pattern on the top using a biscuit stamp. You can also decorate these with a little edible gold glitter on the top or a flaked almond, but I think they are rather pretty just plain and simple.

DRINKS

Sometimes a drink is Biting Biting in itself. A stop by the roadside in India for *masala chai* and a chat, or perhaps some biscuits or *burfi* on the side is enough to help you reset for the day. A glass of milk and an orange becomes an orange milkshake eaten with some *thepla* or a rolled up *rotli* with jaggery for an afternoon treat. And going out for *falooda* on the way home from a wedding because you're feeling that little bit peckish even though you've stuffed yourself with wedding food is a Biting ritual now whenever we are near Wembley. The milk is sweet and soothing and the ice cream is substantial enough to have you complaining again that your saree is way too tight.

Some drinks are also very healing. I often add more fresh ginger to *masala chai* in the winter to ward off colds and when we even had a hint of a cough Mum would give us turmeric milk every evening until that hint was gone.

SALT AND CUMIN-SPICED YOGHURT DRINK

There are some words in Swahili which I never realised were Swahili until I went to India. I remember asking my cousin Reena for an iron. I called it a *pasi* and she didn't have a clue what I was on about as it's *istri* in Gujarati. This is the same for this yoghurt-based drink, which I have always called *chaash* but in India it is commonly known as *lassi*.

Same same <shrugs shoulders>.

Serves 1–2

500ml water
2 heaped tbsp plain yoghurt
½ tsp salt
ground cumin for sprinkling

Whisk the water and yoghurt together with the salt until well combined and serve with a sprinkle of ground cumin. It's really that simple. You can make this thicker or thinner depending on how you like it.

The first time we went to Rajkot as a family we did the rounds of visiting all our family and Dad's friends. It's obligatory. We had been warned to be polite, behave courteously (as if we wouldn't!) and ensure we ate and drank everything given to us so as not to appear rude. The first drink on arrival was always *limbu pani*. It's so hot in August in India and this is the best drink for cooling down – I could have ten in a day and still want more. Each one we were given was ever so slightly different in the ratio of salt and sugar. This is how I like it so do feel free to experiment. It's almost always made by the glass rather than by the jug as this is how we learn the measures.

Serves 2

2 × 500ml glasses of water
juice of 2 large lemons
1 tsp salt
1 tbsp caster sugar (as it dissolves a little faster)
ground cumin or black pepper (optional)

Mix the water, lemon juice, salt and sugar together and stir until the sugar dissolves. Pour back into iced glasses and add a pinch of ground cumin or black pepper if you wish.

On a hot day Dad would be sent out for oranges as this wasn't a fruit we usually had in the house. Mum would spend ages juicing the oranges by hand, crushing ice and then churning the milk and orange juice together with a pinch of salt and black pepper. We didn't have a cocktail shaker or a blender so an empty water bottle did the trick just fine.

Serves 2

2 × 500ml glasses of milk
juice of 3–4 large oranges
1 tsp salt
1 tsp coarse black pepper

Put all the ingredients into a blender and blitz together 'til the orange juice is well combined. If you don't have a blender you can whisk everything together in a large bowl with a hand whisk or use an empty bottle or jar like my mum.

Falooda
ROSE MILKSHAKE

Falooda is my favourite! It reminds me of the little street stalls in Rajkot and the milkman. The family didn't have a fridge when I first visited so Govind Bapa would send for the milkman so I could have this. I remember it being sickly sweet and because I wasn't really allowed very many sweet things as a child (lest my teeth fell out) it was the most delightful thing in the world. Nowadays I find the rose syrup sweet enough but if you want it sweeter do add caster sugar to your taste.

Serves 2

3 tbsp chia or basil seeds
100g vermicelli noodles
600ml milk
4 tbsp rose syrup plus 1 more
    for drizzling
2 scoops vanilla ice cream
2 tbsp chopped pistachios
1 tbsp flaked almonds
hundreds and thousands for
    garnish (optional)

Soak the chia/basil seeds in 50ml water for ten minutes. Cook the vermicelli noodles in boiling water until just tender, then drain and set aside to cool.

To assemble, divide the milk between two large glasses. Into each glass put half of the drained vermicelli noodles and plumped-up chia/basil seeds, and then add two tablespoons of rose syrup into each. Give it a gentle stir. You want to see swirls of the pink syrup.

Add a scoop of vanilla ice cream to each glass and top with the pistachios, almonds and hundreds and thousands. Drizzle with a little rose syrup, add a long spoon and a straw and slurp!

Making tea is a pastime. It's a ritual. A 'time-pass'. While the tea is simmering, you chat, you read, you prepare the Biting you will be having with it – you do something because you're looking at about half an hour of 'time-pass'.

My Dad makes *masala chai* every morning. The proportions of the recipe gets passed down based on the implement used by the individual to measure. My dad uses a mug; my mum a dainty teacup. My cousin Hetal uses a glass about 15cm high. It doesn't really matter what you use as long as the ratio of water to milk is measured the same. The spice mix used is a magic combination individual to the person. Some people now use a ready-made masala but I still make it by adding a bit of this and that depending on my mood.

Serves 2–3

200ml water
400ml milk
1 tbsp Assam or Darjeeling tea
    (or a Twinings English Breakfast
    teabag)
10g fresh ginger
¼ tsp ground cardamom
¼ tsp cinnamon
2 cloves
nutmeg for grating
runny honey or sugar for
    sweetening (optional)

Pour the water into a pan and bring to the boil over a medium heat. Add the milk and the tea or teabag and simmer over a low heat. Stir and add the ginger, cardamom, cinnamon and cloves and then simmer gently for between three and ten minutes depending on how strong you like your tea.

Strain through a tea strainer, grate over a little nutmeg and stir. Sweeten as you wish with honey or sugar. I like to keep stirring as it cools because I don't like the skin that forms on top, but if it does that you can just scoop it out.

TURMERIC LATTE

Hardar Varu Dhoodh

When I had my Library Café in Enfield Town Library I used to make this with foamed milk using the steam wand on the coffee machine and it was absolutely wonderful! A lovely, thick creamy texture that lends itself very well to the pure comfort and joy this drink brings. But you don't need a fancy coffee machine to make this at home, just a good hand whisk and a little elbow grease. It's a wonderful pick-me-up when it's freezing cold outside and you have the sniffles.

Serves 1–2

300ml full fat milk
50ml double cream
1½ tsp turmeric
1 tsp ground ginger
3–4 twists of freshly milled
    black pepper
runny honey for sweetening
    (optional)

Heat the milk and cream in a pan until it is just starting to simmer. Keep this on the lowest heat. Add the turmeric and ground ginger and simmer for five minutes on a low heat, whisking to make it a bit frothy. Pour into a mug and add freshly ground black pepper. I have this as it is, but you can sweeten with honey to your liking.

TONE'S GREEN CHILLI MARGARITA

I had quite a sheltered upbringing and wasn't allowed to go to pubs or bars. Even through university years I didn't really drink alcohol much so it wasn't until I got to Tokyo that I had my first margarita. I lived in Shiinamachi, which had one of the best little Mexican bars near the train station. It was very ramshackle and the owner loved to practise his English. My Tone would sometimes meet me there after work and we'd have Corona beers and margaritas before heading home. After 25 years of marriage Tone knows exactly how I like my margaritas and this version has a lovely little kick.

Serves 2

2–3 tbsp finely crushed sea salt
2–3 small green chillies
3–4 cubes of ice
50ml tequila
50ml Cointreau
50ml fresh lime juice

Put the salt into a flat saucer. Take two Martini glasses or small whisky tumblers and run a wet finger over the rim. Dip the rims into the salt and set aside.

Put the green chillies into a cocktail shaker. Give them a good bashing with a wooden spoon or mortar. Add the ice, tequila, Cointreau and lime juice and then give it a good old shake. You can do a Tone and have a little naff boogie (proper Dad dancing) at the same time. Pour into your prepared glasses and enjoy!

OH NO, MUM'S COMING OVER!

It is customary in our culture to drop in unannounced. I guess it stems from back in India and Tanzania when everyone lived on each other's doorsteps so you could always see who was in and pop over for a good old natter.

My family have continued this 'habit'. We would often get folks popping in to say hello at all times of day because we lived so close to the Wembley shopping area. I think subconsciously Tone and I chose to live away from there after we got married for this exact reason. 'When do you get any peace?! How do they know you'll be home?' he would ask.

If you're home, you're home, and if you're not then they'll come by another time. He still doesn't get it.

This used to happen A LOT when I first had my Amber. I would be mid-shower and Mum would turn up with a few aunties in tow. Soooooo embarrassing as the house would be a total mess which they would all promptly clean and tidy and then proceed to cook.

It has taken me years to train my mum to call or text before she turns up at the house. WhatsApp is the greatest invention ever! So, in case this happens to you, here is a list of go-to recipes you can quickly make to at least give the 'I'm chilled and in control' vibe.

15 Minutes (she's literally around the corner so you only have time to run the Hoover round and get things cooking to finish off as she arrives)

Poppadoms (page 28)
Spiced Puff-pastry Palmiers (page 31)
Spicy Stir-fried Cashews (page 34)
Shaak Chaat (page 80)
Tomato and Onion *Shaak* (page 96)
BBQ Green Bananas (page 136)
Gram Flour Pancakes (page 136)
Cheese and Chevro Sandwich (page 138)
Lemon and Turmeric Spiced Flattened Rice (page 115)
Masala Fried Rice – remember that rice I told you to freeze?
   (page 112)
Cardamom-spiced Yoghurt (page 158)

30 Minutes (she's at home and ready to leave)

Cumin-spiced Cheese on Toast (page 37)
Black Pepper-spiced Cassava (page 44)
Onion, Potato or Spinach and Cheese *Bhajia* with Tomato
   Chutney (page 51)
Mashed Potato Fritters, if you have leftover mash (page 54)
Black-eyed Bean *Bhajia* (page 52)
Steamed Savoury Semolina Cake (page 64)
Rice Flour Dumplings (page 72)
Chickpea, Onion and Potato Salad with Tamarind Chutney
   (page 66)
Stuffed Bullet Chillies (page 94)
Shaak with pitta bread (page 77)
Store Cupboard Tin *Shaak* with rice (page 82)
Dhal Dhokri, if you have leftover dhal (page 106)
Rotli Roll with yoghurt chutney (page 127)
Fenugreek Flatbreads with pickles (page 137)
Dhal Parotha with yoghurt and pickles (page 133)
Spiced *Rotli* Soup (page 130)
Chocolate and Cardamom Mousse (page 165)

45–60 Minutes (Dad's driving)

Shaak with *rotli* and rice (page 77)
Pea Pastries (page 68)
Peanut-stuffed Baby Aubergines (page 86)
Sweetcorn and Cashew Curry (page 93)
Heral's Mum's Cheese and Green Chilli *Parotha* (page 135)
Mum's Sweet Vermicelli (page 156)
Karamsi's Semolina Pudding (page 160)
Brownies (page 164)

INDEX

THANK YOU

My mum's sister Sashi once read my palm. She looked aghast as she delved into the lines and contours and then, annoyingly, she wouldn't share what she had seen. I didn't believe the 'nonsense' then anyway, but I wanted to know why she'd gotten so upset! After much persuasion she told me that I was going to be an outcast. That I would move away from family and traditions and be a distant presence in everyone's lives. Everybody laughed it off of course and I never really thought much of it 'til I was writing this book. I guess marrying a 'white' man, studying and working abroad, living life on my own terms rather than following traditional Indian pathways has kind of realised what she saw back then, but I consider it a blessed life full of opportunities seized.

In the first instance I'd like to give thanks to my late Pappa. From the stories I have heard I think I take after him with that original mindset of wanting something different. Something more. Would I even be here if he hadn't gotten that on the dhow? Would I be more of a traditional Indian girl if I didn't have his obstinance and spirit? Would I have dared travel the world if I didn't have his wanderlust? Who knows but thanks, Pappa, for taking the leap and setting an example for me to follow.

My dad is also incredibly stubborn and set in his ways. He had a single-minded vision to give his family a better life and worked incredibly hard to do that for us. Thanks, Daddy, for getting on that plane to England to increase the opportunities for us to live a fuller life and for instilling the value of learning and hard work.

My mum drove me crazy teaching me to cook when I didn't want to. I'm grateful she did of course but I hated it at the time. Thanks, Mum, for feeding me the best foods growing up and today. You persevered through some pretty tough times in our early years but we never went without a lovingly cooked meal.

There are too many cousins, aunties and uncles to name but I would like to thank Kishore Mama and Gunvanti Mami, Jayanti Mama and Sushila Mami for the generosity of storytelling and photographs of times gone by in Tanzania. Thanks to Dino Bhai for reading with me in those early days in Tooting. You encouraged the gift of language, which I have never forgotten; to Lata Kaki, Pravin Kaka, Amisha, Deepa – you guys are my second home where I can open the fridge freely, knowing you'll always have leftovers and treats for me to pick on; to Pratibha Masi and Lata Kaki for rescuing me on photo shoot day; to Pradeep, Hina, Shabba, Kavita and Dino for beans, chips, *mogo*, apple crumble, Tabasco, espresso Martinis, Malbec, Boxing Day and Gran Canaria.

To my KPMG family for letting me bring my whole self to work — Julio for always listening, unwaveringly championing me and always letting me choose where to eat; Miriam for reminding me that the ladder is always there to climb; Adrian for taking a leap of faith in me back in 2016 and continuously encouraging me to do things differently. To every other KPMGer who has listened to a food-related analogy (and, no, I'm not going to stop them)!

Much thanks to Emily and Nasim at Kitchen Press for believing in this book and for your meticulous attention to detail on every element of the process.

To Matt Inwood for being so patient and bringing these dishes to life through the lens. And for distracting Mum!

To Jenny Linford, Christine Smallwood, Asma Khan and Sabrina Ghayour for many wise words shared over text and Instagram DMs at all times of day.

To my Amber Priya and Amy Sienna for eating everything I cook (except maybe that tomato ice cream — sorry!). I hope you take these recipes forward to keep our culture and memories alive.

Finally, to my Tone for lifting me up since the day we met.

Thank you.

Urvashi x

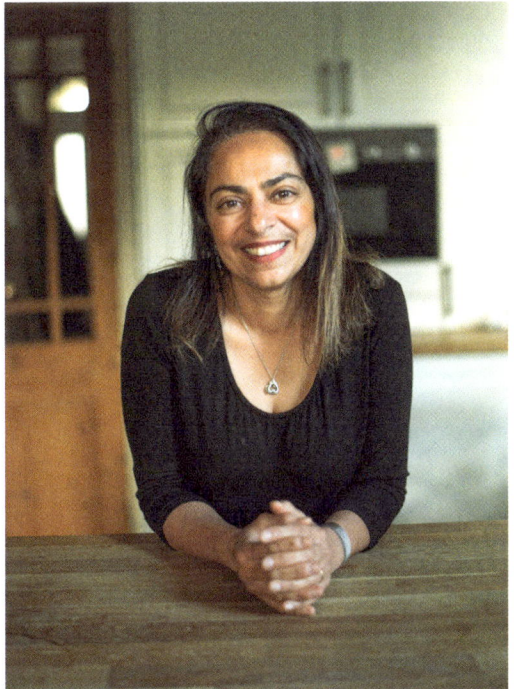

Published in 2022 by Kitchen Press Ltd,
1 Windsor Place, Dundee, DD2 1BG
www.kitchenpress.co.uk

Distributed in Australia and New Zealand by
David Bateman Ltd

Text © Urvashi Roe
Photography © Matt Inwood
Illustrations by Patrick Hughes
Text design by Clare Skeats
Illustration on page 14 by Jen Collins

ISBN 978 1 9163165 9 1

A CIP catalogue record for this book is available from
the British Library.

Printed in Malta

10 9 8 7 6 5 4 3 2 1